IFISM
Vol. 3

The Complete works of
ORUNMILA

THE ODUS OF OYEKU-MEJI

C. Osamaro Ibie

B.Sc Econs (Hon) London, B.A. Econs (Hons)
Strathclyde FIAMN (Hons) CDA (Hons)

IFISM VOL. 3

Copyright by C. OSAMARO IBIE

2024 reprint edition by Blacklegacypress.org

All Rights Reserved.

ISBN: 978-1-63652-433-7

Contents

		Pages
Chapter 1	Agbigba or Oguega	1 - 8
Chapter 2	Oyeku - yi - Logbe	9 - 13
Chapter 3	Oyeku - bi - Iwori	14 - 17
Chapter 4	Oyeku - si - Idi	18 - 23
Chapter 5	Oyeku - Obara	25 - 28
Chapter 6	Oyeku - Okonron	29 - 34
Chapter 7	Oyeku - bi - Irosun	35 - 39
Chapter 8	Oyeku - bo - Owanrin	40 - 44
Chapter 9	Oyeku - Ogunda	45 - 51
Chapter 10	Oyeku - Osa	52 - 57
Chapter 11	Oyeku - Etura	58 - 69
Chapter 12	Oyeku - bi - Irete	70 - 75
Chapter 13	Oyeku - be - Eka	76 - 80
Chapter 14	Oyeku - le - Eturukpon	81 - 87
Chapter 15	Oyeku - Ose	88 - 96
Chapter 16	Oyeku - Ofun	97 - 100

Prologue To Volume III

Orunmila has revealed that when God created the divinities and man, He intended that success was to be measured in terms of one's contributions to the objective good. The barometer for measuring such contributions was expected to be the degree of harmony, co-operation and love fostered among his creatures. On the other hand Esu was determined to substitute these goals with discord, confrontation and hatred, as the values of a self-centred world.

Moreover, Orunmila will reveal that "money" and "power" became the tantalizers held out by Esu for manipulating and teleguiding the human psyche and soul. The quest for these subjective values provided Esu the parameters with which he constructed an anthropocentric universe, a factor which became largely responsible for the capriciousness of earthly values and standards, as human history reveals.

In this and subsequent books, the author will endeavour to present a bird's-eye-view of how money has affected human socio-political and religious institutions in the last two thousand years, since man engaged himself in the search for the meaning of life on earth.

Since the attention of thinkers moved from the study of man in a state of nature to the study of man in society, one fact has been irrefutable, which is, that man has not succeeded in his vain attempt to build a paradise on earth. History has reflected man's attempts to solve the problem of survival through brute force, cheating, robbery, customs and command behind a facade of central governance.

Starting with the feudal system in which man was enslaved by traditional usage and command by head chiefs, Lords, the aristocracy of birth and wealth and kings, man tried to manumit himself by changing to a society in which survival came to depend on leaving the individual to be free to organise his life as he pleased in what came to be known as the Laissez-Faire approach to societal management. It subsequently turned out to be the institutionalization of the contrivance of Esu to cut men adrift in order to divide and rule them instead of allowing them to cooperate with one another to optimise the general good of all. It also set the stage which allowed the few hundreds or thousands to become outrageously rich at the expense of the impoverished millions of people. The inequitable attributes of that system culminated in the creation of a class structure in society made up of the "haves" and the "have-nots".

The Laissez-Faire concept created such a furore of discontent in human governance that its protagonists renovated it with the more phlegmatic gloss of "the Market System". Under the market system, the propensity to maximize personal gains at the expense of the less privileged majority became the axis around which individual and societal efforts revolved. The proponents of the acquisitive pull argued that by allowing individuals to be free to maximise their greed, the interest of society writ-large will be safe-guarded. The profit nexus became the hub-house of human eco-political stimulus.

Right from its outset, the exotic market system was held by the defenceless majority with suspicion and distrust, because the antediluvian biblically-inspired "Usury Laws" under which millions of people were decimated for "the heinous crime of making profit especially from money lending" still held sway. On its part, the church subsequently subsequently sanctified the Usury Laws in 1830 after condemning it for 1,000 years and that was when itself.

The philosophy of wealth at all cost brought with it a new social problem. According to Heilbroner in his book on "The worldly philosophers", the problem became "how to keep the poor to (remain) poor." The political arithmeticians of the eighteenth century generally advocated that "unless the poor were kept poor, they could not be counted upon to do an honest day's toil without asking for exorbitant wages." A leading moralist wrote in 1723 that "To make society happy, it is necessary that great numbers should be wretched as well as poor." Another school advocated that "the poor were meant by God to be poor and even if they were not, their poverty was essential to the wealth of the nation." That was a reverberation of Aristotle's dictum of 300 BC that "From the hour of their birth some are marked out for subjection and some for command."

Beginning with the wonderful world pictured by Adam Smith in his book on "the Wealth of Nations" in 1776, through the gloomy world of Parson Malthus and David Ricardo, the beautiful world of the Utopian socialists, right up to the inexorable world of Karl Marx, the melee of eco-philosophical argument was how to salvage the poor working class from the ugly excesses of the capitalists. History is today repeating itself which is why this matter has found expression in an abstract book on Ifism. How man used the quest for profit to subjugate, de-humanise, rob, aggress, and destabilize his fellow men nationally and internationally will be the prologue to the next and subsequent books, in order to demonstrate the dictum that MONEY is the root of all evils.

Written by:
MR. C. OSAMARO IBIE RETIRED FEDERAL PERMANENT SECRETARY *B.Sc. Econs. (Hons.) London B.A. Econs (Hons.) Strathclyde FIAMN (Hon.) CDA (Hon.)*

God brought out a large container of wild melons and gave one to each of the contestants, while giving two to Ominigun. God told all of them to reassemble in His Outer Chamber on the fifth day and to appear in their ceremonial regalias because He was going to make an important proclamation. He wanted to use that occasion to proclaim the appointment of Ominigun as a divinity. God also sent one melon to Orunmila through his colleagues and told them to direct him not to fail to attend the next conference, having sent a message on that occasion that he was serving his Ifa. It is commonly known that Orunmila does not move out of his house on the day he serves his Ifa.

All the divinities, including Ominigun trouped to Orunmila's house to give him God's message and to verify whether in truth, he was serving his Ifa. They arrived at his house to discover that he had prepared the table for a sumptuous feast. Without waiting to be invited, they all sat down to eat and drink to their heart's content. It was not until they had enjoyed his hospitality, that they delivered God's message to Orunmila. He was very happy to receive the melon because he needed it to serve his Ifa.

When the others saw how happy he was to receive the melon, they all surrendered their's to him because they said that they did not know how to eat melon. He expressed his profound gratitude to them after which they dispersed.

The following morning, Akpetebi (Orunmila's wife) asked him where the food for the day was going to come from, since he had used all the foodstuff and money in the house for the previous day's feast. He replied that she could be cooking out of the melons until clients came in. When she took out one of the melons to cut up for cooking, she noticed a metallic sound from within it. She was surprised to see that the melon was laden with beads and money. She quickly called Orunmila to see what she had discovered. The entire consignment of melons, yielded beads and money which filled a whole room in the house. Orunmila had been translated into unforeseen wealth and prosperity. That is why when Ofun-Ogbe comes out for a person during Ifa initiation ceremony at Ugbodu, he is often advised not to part with any gift given to him by a higher authority no matter how unappealing it may seem. The person is bound to be prosperous by a stroke of fortune.

Meanwhile, Orunmila bought a horse, prepared a beaded dress for himself and the horse complete with cap and shoes to match, against the next invitation of God.

On the appointed day, God had prepared a second throne and positioned it close to his Divine Throne and earmarked it to be occupied by the best-dressed invitee to the conference. In fact since God gave two melons to Ominigun, He intended him to have the means of funding the best attire and for him to occupy the second throne before upgrading him to the status of a divinity.

One after the other the divinities appeared at the conference chamber and took their seats. Ominigun also came in his usual rags and sat on the floor. God was surprised to see him. At that morning's divination, Orunmila had been told to make sure that he was the last to arrive at the conference. As soon as he made sure that all the other invitees were already seated, he got dressed in his new beaded regalia and rode on his horse with a beaded flywhisk in hand to the conference chamber. As soon as he alighted from the horse, he was given a spontaneous ovation and after genuflecting to greet God, he was motioned to take the second seat by the side of God. Almost instantaneously, the other divinities acclaimed Orunmila, as Orisa-Keji, that is, the next divinity to God, which he does not often like to be called.

As soon as all were assembled, God observed that no other divinity was adorned with beads except Orunmila. He then asked the others what they did with the melons he gave them at the previous meeting. They all announced in unison that since He gave them no entertainment during the day-long meeting, they feasted in Orunmila's house after the meeting, and since he needed it to serve his Ifa, they surrendered their own to him en-masse. After a deep reflection, God proclaimed that for parting with the "Food" he gave them, they should from then on forbid the eating of melon, with the exception of the divinity of wisdom, Orunmila.

God then brought out His divine instrument of authority and proclaimed that any divinity who ate melon would from that day lose his power and authority (ASE). He next turned to Ominigun and told him that forever and from then on, he would always go in rags unless he sought solace under the cover of Orunmila, and that he would always sit on the floor to be able to foretell and divine. That is why to this day, an Agbigba (Oguega) diviner can only prosper if he has his own Ifa. On that note, the conference dispersed.

It is for this reason that some adherents of Ifa refer to Orunmila as Orisa-Keji (the next to God). But Orunmila has warned the writer never to refer to him as Orisa-Keji because God did not proclaim it on that day. God only referred to him as the Divinity of wisdom, apparently for successfully using the law of unintended consequences to obtain from the other divinities the gifts He gave to them. God never revealed to the other divinities and Ominigun, the significance of the Divine gifts they parted with.

That was how Ominigun lost the only opportunity of being up-graded to the rank of a divinity, and why it is said that any divinity that eats wild melon loses his or her authority.

ORUNMILA BUYS OMINIGUN AS A SLAVE

The curse on Ominigun was later to manifest when he subsequently fell from Grace to Grass. Try as he did to make ends meet, he could not. One night, his guardian angel appeared to him in a dream and told him that since the curse of God was on him, his only salvation lay in going to the market to offer himself for sale as a slave.

He hesitated for sometime, since he was not given to going for divination. When things became really difficult for him, he eventually decided to obey the injunction of his guardian angel. He had been warned by his guardian angel that his fortunes would always undulate by rising and falling, unless he had his own Ifa. Having demonstrated that he was a more proficient seer, he had always looked down on Orunmila and wondered how he could condescend to request him to prepare Ifa for him.

At one of his morning divinations, Orunmila was told to offer a he-goat to Esu to avoid the danger of buying a slave that could outshine and subvert him. He made the sacrifice without delay. On the next market day, he went to the market as usual. After getting to his stall, he began his work. As he was divining for some one, in came a slave who offered himself for sale to a willing buyer. The slave looked very active and well built. Orunmila quickly offered to buy him. After paying him the asking price, Orunmila told him to sit down and wait to accompany him home at the close of the market.

Meanwhile, Orunmila went into the market to buy some materials he was to take home for his work, but before returning from his shopping spree, the slave had disappeared. When Orunmila returned to his stall, he asked after the slave he had just bought and his neighbours told him that they thought the man had accompanied him in his shopping. In vain, he went in search of the slave. He then sounded his Ifa who told him that, that was the slave against whom he was advised to make the sacrifice he made before coming to the market. He was told not to worry because he would meet the slave waiting for him at home.

True to the manifestation of his market divination, he actually met the slave waiting for him at home. Asked how he knew the way to Orunmila's house, the slave declared that he saw the way to Orunmila's home from his sitting position in the market and thought it was best to come and wait for him at home to prepare for his return. With that, Orunmila was left in no doubt regarding the potentialities of this strange slave.

As soon as he settled down, Orunmila asked for his name and he gave it as Ominigun (OMINIGBON in Bini). Meanwhile, he explained to Orunmila how he lost all his heavenly belongings and began to go in rags and to beg for food to eat. When he subsequently went for divination, he was told that his only salvation lay in getting himself to be bought as a slave. That was how he came to the market to be bought up as a slave. Orunmila immediately invited Akpetebi, his wife to treat Ominigun with the reverence he deserved and not to treat him as a slave because he was a person of substance.

The following morning, some people were coming to Orunmila's house for divination and without seeing them, Ominigun declared from the interior of the house that there were three persons coming to Orunmila for divination and he mentioned the problems each of them wanted to resolve through divination as well as telling them what sacrifices they were to make.

The practice of pre-empting Orunmila to divine for his visitors became so regular that very soon no one bothered to listen to Orunmila's long process of divination anymore. Callers began to prefer the instant divination of Ominigun. Besides, he was in the habit of staging dance demonstrations every eight days at which he exhibited his diabolical prowess. He was capable of standing on his ears and dancing to the delight of spectators whilst at the same time divining for them without using any instruments. He was also capable of severing his head from his body while both parts danced separately to be joined together in the air. He had clearly outshone his master, who was beginning to suffer from lack of patronage since all his previous clients swung to his supposed slave. Unfortunately, Ominigun's ephemeral success beclouded his vision and he never bothered to ask Orunmila to prepare Ifa for him. That is why, to this day, it is well nigh impossible for an Agbigba diviner to endure in prosperity unless he is discreet enough to have his own Ifa.

Ominigun had come to make so much money from his performances and divination that he was able to put up several imposing buildings and halls around his master's residence. People were beginning to wonder whether Orunmila was indeed the master of Ominigun, who had tacitly but clearly, stolen the show from his master.

While Orunmila took the situation with equanimity, Esu was poised to intervene on the side of Orunmila. At the next dancing session, Ominigun was again demonstrating to the delight of his spectators. Once again, he severed his head from the rest of his body and while his body was dancing on the ground, his head was dancing in the air. Meanwhile, Esu seized his head and took it into the air never to return to his body. After the body had danced for sometime without the head to keep it together, the body fell to the ground, dead. That was the end of Ominigun in heaven. He subsequently left for the world without his head, which explains why he has no shrine and no distinct mode of worship. Orunmila then inherited all of Ominigun's belongings, being his master.

OMINIGBON EMERGES ON EARTH

The divinities had meanwhile abandoned the earth to mankind. There was a place called Ibere-aiye or Eziagbon, which was later to be called Ugodomigodo and subsequently Ile-Ibinu or Benin. Orunmila has revealed that it was at Ibere-aiye (Eziagbon) he first landed and settled briefly, but later moved to settle at Uhe which was subsequently called Ile-Ife.

The first human inhabitants of Ibere-aiye (Eziagbon) were Etebite and his wife Eteghori. They had established a habitation at Eziagbon and it expanded tremendously. Following his demise in heaven, Ominigbon appeared on earth as a male child in the household of Etebite. As he grew up, his parents noticed that he was able to foretell upcoming events with precision. He was able to warn prospective victims about the imminent approach of danger and how to avert it. Whenever death targetted a victim on earth, Ominigbon would warn the person and advise him on the precautionary moves to make. His proficiency as a seer soon brought him in contact with the royalty. He was often invited to divine for the royal household and he invariably did so quite satisfactorily. Nonetheless, the unparalleled efficacy of his divining was to put him at odds with more experienced and elderly diviners.

At the same time, his pre-emptive moves were beginning to annoy the divinities, especially Death. He also incurred the displeasure of Esu because his peculiar mode of divination negated the offer of sacrifice to the divinity of evil. Meanwhile, Death had sent messengers from heaven to come and fetch the King of Eziagbon from the earth.

As soon as Death's messengers took off from heaven, he went to the palace to warn the King that Death was on his trail. He advised the King to prepare an elaborate feast for visitors who were due in the palace the following day.

The King adhered to the advice of Ominigbon and prepared food and drinks for a palace feast the following day. Among those invited to the feast was Ominigbon himself. At about noon, seven men arrived at the palace but before they could deliver their message, they were invited to participate in the feasting.

At about sunset, the leader of the seven visitors introduced himself and revealed the purpose of their mission. He disclosed that he was told to invite the King to heaven. Since there is no appeal against the injunctions of Death, the King agreed to embark on the journey that evening. It was the turn of Ominigbon to intervene. He confronted the heavenly visitors and asked them why they dared to enjoy the hospitality of the King if they were going to terminate his life on earth. He reminded them of the heavenly law which precludes Death from killing anyone, after eating his or her food. On that note the visitors left the palace and returned to heaven without the King. Before leaving, they proclaimed that whoever forewarned the King and advised him to feed them pre-emptively would carry the yoke of the King's death.

That night, there was general rejoicing in the royal household after which all the local invitees retired to their respective homes. On getting home Ominigbon, otherwise called Oguega in Eziagbon, invited the members of his family and told them that he was about to leave them for good. He told his eldest son Ogbeide that he would impart his art of divination to him after his return to heaven. Ominigbon went to bed but did not wake up the following morning. His death was reported to the King who ordered that he should be given a royal funeral. He was buried in his courtyard.

THE ORIGIN OF OGUEGA OR AGBIGBA AS A MODE OF DIVINATION

A few weeks after the death of Ominigbon, his son Ogbeide observed that a plant had germinated on the grave of his father. The plant soon began to flower, and to bear fruits. When the fruits became ripe, they fell to the ground. On seeing the dried shells of the fallen fruits, the son, Ogbeide was able to see beyond what the ordinary eyes could see. By gazing into the shells he was immediately endowed with the power to foretell up-coming events.

Ogbeide kept the secret to himself because he realised that it was the manifestation of his father's last proclamation of transferring his art of divination to him. Ogbeide soon became very popular as a seer and diviner and his fame reached the King who was told that Ogbeide had developed all the mysterious attributes of his father. The king decided to invite him along with other diviners and seers for a proficiency test.

At the same time an Ifa priest was operating in Eziagbon. His name was Ogbe-Ate. He was earlier invited by the king to Eziagbon to save the life of his eldest son from the cult of witchcraft. Ogbe-Ate had done what other divine priests in Eziagbon could not do, by saving the life of the crown prince of Eziagbon. The king asked Ogbe-Ate whether he would agree to a proficiency contest with other divine priests and seers in his kingdom. His initial reaction was to decline the invitation, but when he consulted Ifa subsequently, he was told to agree to participate in the contest, provided he gave a he-goat to Esu. Subsequently, he went to the palace to inform the king that he was ready for the contest.

All the divine priests and witch-doctors of Eziagbon, together with Ogbeide were invited for the contest. The Ifa priest, Ogbe-Ate was also invited for the contest. Ogbe-

Ate lost no time in making the sacrifice to Esu.

Meanwhile, the king of Eziagbon ordered 100 men and 100 women to be incarcerated, in separate apartments for keeping prisoners of war, without disclosing the purpose of the exercise to anyone.

After eating the he-goat offered by Ogbe-Ate, Esu went late in the night to the location of the female internees and induced into labour one of the women who was at an advanced stage of pregnancy. The woman delivered a male child before dawn.

Later that morning, all the invited guests and contestants were assembled. The king was the last to take his seat. As soon as he was seated, he revealed that he was anxious to proclaim the most proficient seer in his kingdom. In that connection he had kept certain materials in separate locations. He added that the first seer, priest or diviner to declare the aggregate contents of the two places would be given the title of the High priest of the Kingdom of Eziagbon (or Ibere-Aiye).

While others were still fidgeting with and rattling their divination instruments, Ogbeide, the son of Ominigbon stepped forward and revealed that the King had kept 100 men and 100 women in confinement since the previous evening. Others declared all sorts of things which were wide off the mark. It was the turn of Ogbe-Ate to speak. At divination, his own ODU came out and he chanted the relevant incantation, "that God (Olodumare) created the 200 divinities (Ugba Erumale), but that Esu infiltrated them. Since the King wanted to know the aggregate number of materials he kept in the two locations, he had the authority of Orunmila, the divinity of Wisdom to proclaim that there were 201 human beings under confinement.

The King who nodded his head approvingly when Ogbeide made his declaration began to show signs of uneasiness. After all the contestants had taken their turns, it was time for the king to declare the winner. Before doing so however, he decided to send two verifiers to each of the two chambers and to report their findings.

The two men who went to verify the male chamber declared that they counted 100 men. On the other hand, those who went to verify the female chamber disclosed that they counted 100 women and one newly born child. Although all eyes had turned on Ogbeide as the winner, it was eventually the visiting Ifa priest Ogbe-Ate, that became the cynosure of all eyes.

Ogbeide felt so disappointed that he conceded supremacy to Ogbe-Ate. Since Ogbe-Ate was only a visiting Ifa priest and not a citizen of Ibere-Aiye, he declined to accept appointment as the Chief Priest of the Kingdom. He offered it to Ogbeide who was equally correct in his disclosure. At that point the king intervened that without the participation of Ogbe-Ate, he would have declared Ogbeide the winner of the contest because he actually ordered 100 men and 100 women to be kept in confinement overnight. The king gave adequate compensation to Ogbe-Ate who was due to return to Uhe (now Ife) soon afterwards.

Baffled at the exactitude with which Ogbe-Ate made his declaration, Ogbeide offered to learn from the former, his art of Ifa divination. That was how the similarity between the 256 ODUS of Ifa and Oguega (Agbigba) came about as may be verified from the sixteen principal ODUS.

S/NO.	NAMES OF IFA'S ODUS	NAMES OF OGUEGA'S ODUS
1.	OGBE	OGBI
2.	OYEKU	AKO
3.	IWORI	OGHORI
4.	EDI	ODIN
5.	OBARA	OBA
6.	OKONRON	OKAN
7.	IROSUN	ORUHU
8.	OWANRIN	OGHAE
9.	EGITAN	IGHITAN
10.	OSA	OHA
11.	ETURA	ETURE
12.	IRETE	ETE
13.	EKA	EKA
14.	ETURUKPON	EROKHUA
15.	OSE	OSE
16.	OFUN	OHUN

Chapter 2

THE ODUS OF OYEKU

OYEKU-YI-LOGBE
```
I    II
I    II
I    II
I    II
```

When this Odu comes out at Ugbodu, the person should be told that his fortune resides near the sea or a big river. If he is not already living near the water, the quest for the means of livelihood will take him there and he should settle there for the rest of his life. As soon as possible, he should prepare an image of the Water divinity (Oshun in Yoruba and Olokun in Bini) for his Ifa shrine because he will derive a lot of benefits from that divinity.

Heavenly works of Oyeku-yi-logbe: He made divination for the three brothers of the Serpent Kindred:

The Python, Boa and Adder were born of the same parents. They went to Orunmila for divination when they were coming to the world. Oyeku-yi-logbe came out for them at divination. The Boa was the senior and the eldest of the three sons. The Boa is called Oka in Yoruba or Arunmwoto in Bini. The second one in order of seniority was the Python or Boa constrictor. It is called Ere in Yoruba and Ikpin in Bini. The most junior was the Adder or Viper who is called 'Kparamole'.. in Yoruba or 'Ivbiekpo' in Bini.

Orunmila advised each of them to serve; his head with a goat, and Esu with a he-goat, and together they were to contribute money to buy a goat to serve their late father. Whoever this Odu comes out for at Ugbodu is the son of Oshun or Olokun and he should be asked whether he has two other brothers in his family. He is likely to be the second son of a family of three sons. If he makes the above sacrifice, he will surely prosper tremendously.

The Python persuaded the others to let them perform the sacrifices but the other two refused. Orunmila had advised them that if they made sacrifice, the Boa would become the King of the thicket, while the Python would become the king of the sea and the Viper would become the king of the open forest. The Boa however served his head with a hen, served Esu with a small chicken and his father with kolanut and wine. The Python on the other hand, served; his head with a goat, Esu with he-goat, and used a cock to promise a goat to his father since the others refused to join hands with him to buy a goat. The Adder made no sacrifice at all.

The three children have their individual instruments of authority (ASE). At the time they went to Orunmila for divination, he was making a sacrifice to his Ifa with a goat, hen, a rat and wine all of which he bought on credit. At that point, the creditors were with Orunmila to demand the payment of the debts he owed them. The sight of the creditors and their indomitable disposition to the instant payment of their debts, provoked the three visitors/divinees and they instantly went into action. The Python attacked the goat seller while the Boa attacked the hen seller and the Viper attacked the seller of rat and wine and they all died instantaneously leaving their debts unpaid. That is why when this Odu comes out at divination, the person is told not to draw the debts or credit owed to him to avoid the danger of losing his life in the process.

Thereafter, the Viper left to settle on the grass land (`Ato' in Bini and `Kpakpa'... in Yoruba). The Boa went to settle in the thicket of the forest while the Python went to settle in the swamps of the sea.

The Viper could not have enough to feed on in the grass land except on insects and did not grow beyond a length of 12 inches. On his part, the Boa could only live on rats which is the equivalent of the chicken with which he make sacrifice to Esu. He does not grow beyond a size of 2 1/2 to 3 feet.

The Boa constrictor who made full sacrifice, had enough to eat on the swamps and grew to the size at which it could swallow animals as big as a goat, big fishes and other reptiles on the swamps. That is why it is able to grow up to a length size of 100 to 300 feet. After he had grown to full size in the swamps, the decided to come out to the white sand on the shore of the sea to sun-bath. As the rays of the sun beamed on his silvery colour formation, it was glittering under the noon day sun. Meanwhile, one of Olokun's servants came out for an errand from under the depth of the sea and saw this huge and long shinning object not before seen in the entire prescint of the water. The servant ran back into the sea to tell the divinity of the sea (Oshun or Olokun) that he had seen a tall handsome man with a shinning body on her sand bed. Olokun decided to go and see for herself. When she saw the attractive and handsome body of the Boa constrictor, she was astonished. When she called on him, he wanted to escape but Olokun persuaded him not to run but to follow her. She took him home to become her husband which made him to become the very personification of prosperity. That was how the Boa constrictor got to its present disposition as a reward for the full sacrifice he made.

It will be observed that the three brothers of the Serpent family have the same colour scheme, and it was the sacrifice which they made or did not make, that is responsible for their differing sizes.

How Oyeku-yi-logbe came to the world:

Before coming to the world, he was known in heaven as Omo oni ghorogbo Orun, that is the celestial reformer because of his magnanimous and liberal disposition. To be able to continue with his benevolent practices on earth, he went to an awo called Oshinu akpo yorun-aroni maja. He was determined to make the world a better place. He was told; to make sacrifice with a guinea fowl, a pigeon, to make a feast of akara to the small children of heaven, and to give he-goat to Esu. He did all the sacrifices and came to the world to continue work as an Ifa priest in earnest.

One day, there was a cholera epidemic on earth which was taking the lives of so many infants. Without being invited, he collected all the leaves for healing cholera attack, and began to go from house to house to administer it to all the victims of the epidemic. Within a matter of days, the epidemic abated and all its victims became well. Not long afterward, there was a spate of high fever and convulsion among children which he also cured. By this time he had firmly established himself as a physician and paediatrician.

Soon afterward, he returned to heaven to report on his experience on earth to the council of the divinities. After reporting on how he was able to heal the sick, make the barren to bear children and the blind to see, God renamed him, Omo onighorogbo aye after which He blessed and cleared him to return to the world to continue his good work. He succeeded on earth immensely with the support of Esu and the elders of the night. He came to have several surrogates who supported him in his works.

The works of his Surrogates:

They advised Oye lugbada and Oye lugbudu to make sacrifices for successful marriage and prosperity.

Ogun kori, Ote koja was his surrogate who made divination for Alaran Oyiyi Omo abeigun fara yira when death was hovering round him. He was told to offer he-goat to the king of Death who then left him alone to flourish in the world. When this Odu portends the danger of death (Ayeo), the person is advised to offer a he-goat to the king of Death at a road junction.

Akeke ni gegi jaale was another of his surrogates who made divination and sacrifice for Shaake in order to have his instrument of authority (Ashe). The Ifa priests have a special way of preparing the Ashe of this Odu. Whatever the user of the Ashe commands with it, will manifest within a span of 24 hours. That is in commemoration of the special Ashe which God gave him before his second trip to the world. The instruments for preparing the Ashe cannot find space in this book. It is the exclusive preserve of the Ifa priest.

Ashe beere was his favourite colleague who in heaven made divination and sacrifice for Agbe or Awe, a red feathered bird, before he succeeded in marrying a woman called Ulukori.

He made divination for two brothers:

There lived two brothers at Ife called Kiwuru and Kuwuwu. They both had only one loin cloth which they wore in turns. Their profession was fetching of firewood for sale from the forest. They used to go out to the forest together to fetch firewood. But only one of them could go out in their cloth to sell the wood in the market, while the other stayed nude in-doors. One day, one of them was ill and he stayed indoors, while the other went alone to fetch firewood in the forest. The sick one used their cloth to cover his body. Before the one who went to the forest returned, the sick one died. Neighbours thought it would be wrong to leave his interment to his brother. They therefore arranged to bury the dead one with the only cloth they both had.

When the other brother returned from the forest he was told of the death and burial of his brother. The neighbours did not know that they buried the deceased with th[e] cloth they both had. After dusk, the living brother went to the grave where hi[s] brother was buried and exhumed his corpse to remove their only loin cloth. As removing the cloth from the grave, he observed a shining objects. As he dug furth[er] the grave, he found more of the shining objects. As he dug deep into the ground, h[e found] a chest containing gold and diamond which at that time were unknown to manki[nd. He] took the chest home to become the first goldsmith that the world ever knew. Fr[om this] discovery, his fortune was transformed from penury to affluence. He began to p[roduce] gold and diamond ornamentations for the royalty and the aristocracy. Kuwuwu w[as the] first goldsmith to cast crowns in gold and diamond in the known world of the t[ime].

When this Odu comes out at divination for a destitute or pauper, he should be [told to] make a special sacrifice with a goat which would be buried in the ground after wh[ich he] is bound to become affluent. He should be advised not to take any oath for any p[urpose] whatsoever. The sacrifice is prepared by putting the head of the goat, 2 pigeons, 2 [and] the head of a pig, sheer-butter (Ori-oyo) into a new pot with the appropriate leave[s and] buried on the floor of the house where he lives, with the following incantations:

    Ifa Oyeku-lo-gbe,
    Ise ori ran mi ni mo nje,
    Ona orisa-nla ni mo nto,
    Mo tono titi mo de ilu okoro jako,
    Mogbo gudu gudu agba ni ile enifo,
    Agba ni onifo nda ni ojo jomo ni ile re,
    Mo gbo kekere ipesi ni mo ya'lowo,
    Ipesi ni a nfi ki olo-Arere gun-jin,
    Omo aro korodoro agbe olu aje wa si ile,
    Mo gbo jinrin-jingin ni mo ya l'agbede,
    Ire mogun-omo-alagbede akoko.

HE MADE DIVINATION FOR THE CHAMELEON
    Sheku Sheku agba,
    Oto ero, Adifa fun Alagemo,
    Nijo ti ofe loja fun Olodumare,
    Ebo ishegun lo'nru o.

When an elderly person is going to embark on a project bigger than himself and pe[ople] are doubting his ability to accomplish the task, he can only succeed through sacrif[ice].

These were the names of the Awos who made divination for the chameleon (Alage[mo] in Yoruba or Omaen-n'erokhi in Bini) when he was going to challenge Olokun on bel[half] of God. The chameleon was the oldest servant in the divine house-hold of God.

He was present on the day when Olokun, the divinity of Water and wealth, ov[er] reached himself by boasting that he was richer than God. God reminded Olokun t[hat] He, was his creator and that whatever he had, belonged to Him. Olokun replied the[t he] recognised that generic fact, but argued that if a creature or a son becomes richer his creator of Father, the latter must admit as a matter of fact, that the former has prospered more than himself. Olokun added that it was a mark of progress when a son became more prosperous than the father and that the father should have the courtesy to admit the fact. Since Olokun held on to his point, God agreed that he should come and demonstrate his wealth in seven days time.

As soon as Olokun left, God gave special authority to the chameleon to challenge Olokun. God had earlier conferred on the chameleon the power to replicate any scenario. Nonetheless, the chameleon decided to go for divination to Orunmila who advised him to make sacrifice and he did.

On the appointed day, the chameleon sat on the throne next to God and told Olokun that God had authorised him to take on his challenge because, He, considered it infra dig for Him to compete or contest with his creature.

Olokun came in, dressed in gorgeously designed white apparel and wearing a beaded crown. As soon as he sat down, everything he wore appeared on the body of the chameleon. Olokun was puzzled. He dressed up 14 times but all appeared on the body of the chameleon. Olokun had exhausted all his dresses and the chameleon had not eve started. Dejected and deflated, Olokun conceeded to God and accepted that he acted contempt of the Almighty Father, for which he profoundly apologised.

At divination, if Ure, the person should be told to make sacrifice in order to accomp a seemingly impossible task. If it is Ayewo, he should be warned not to act in conte of, or to challenge an authority greater than himself, because he will be disgrace

DIVINATION FOR ORUNMILA AGAINST ENMITY:

	Akere olodo olu,
	Orun, kii'waye, warojo,
Meaning:	The frog inside the river or heaven,
	Does not return to the world,
	To quarrel or fight.

That was the Awo who made divination for Orunmila when six enemies from different sources rose to fight him. He was told to make sacrifice to Esu with a he-goat, rat, fish, eko and akara and to serve Ifa with a ram. He made the sacrifices.

Thereafter, when the enemies came to wage war on him, Esu made them to dance in praise of Orunmila.

At divination for a man, he should be told to make sacrifice because, he is surrounded by six enemies, one of who is planning to seduce his wife. For a woman, she should be told that six men who unsuccessfully woed her are planning to undo her. She uld make sacrifice to neutralize their machinations.

Chapter 3

OYEKU-BI-IWORI

```
OYEKU-BIRI
I I   I I
I     I I
I     I I
I I   I I
```

Oyeku-bi-wori was famous in heaven for making divination for all divinities, mortals, animals and birds, alike. He used to hold meetings with all of them on different occasions. He started by holding meetings with the birds (night witches). The meeting was always held in his house. The convener/manager of the meetings was a bird called saaro in Yoruba and Esiasio in Bini. To this day, that bird otherwise called "the convener", continues to play the role of convening meetings of the birds of the air. Oyeku-bi-wori subsequently also arranged to hold meetings with the animals of the forest. The bush pig (Tukpu in Yoruba and Esi-oha in Bini) was appointed convener of the meetings of mammals. At each meeting with the birds and animals, he used to make divination for the two groups on how to avoid the evil machinations of their enemies.

Meanwhile, Ogun decided to befriend Oyeku-biri as a strategy for getting at the birds and animals. As a hunter, Ogun was no longer recording much success in his hunting expedition on account of the regular sacrifices that his potential victims were making with the help of Orunmila.

One day, Ogun made a clean breast of his intentions and told Orunmila that he was preparing for his annual festival and sought his advice on the animals he was going to kill for the celebration. Oyeku-biri asked Ogun for what he had in mind and he disclosed that he required Saaro and Tukpu for his sacrificial victims. They happened to be the two conveners of the meetings of the birds and animals. Ogun however complained that he had the problem of knowing how to meet them in their homes. Oyeku-biri told Ogun that it was no problem. He advised him that at the next meeting of the birds, if he heard silu silu eye oribo, two times, he should come to the venue of the meeting. That was the call sign of Saaro which would be an indication that he was at home. On the other hand if he heard Ode-yo-okpaa tukpu eemona eron igbofo, being the call sign of Tukpu, it would be an indication that he was at home.

When Ogun asked for the date of the next meeting, Oyeku-biri indicated that it would be in seventeen days' time (Itadogun). But Orunmila had no intention of betraying his clients. He subsequently advised the two groups to offer he-goat to Esu and to dig a bunker underneath the room where they held their meetings. They did as they were advised.

On the day of the meeting, Saaro and Tukpu convened the meeting after they had taken cover in the bunker. When Ogun heard the call signs he left for the venue of the meeting. On getting there, he met Oyeku-biri alone at the venue. Oyeku-biri told him that for the first time, Saaro had convened a meeting which did not hold, much against the dictum that Saaro or Esiasio does not convene a meeting that does not hold. Oyeku-biri however asked Ogun to sit down. Unknown to him, the birds and animals had dug a concealed trench beneath the chair on which Ogun was sitting. As soon as he sat down, he fell into the hole and the fire started burning. At that point, all the birds and animals ran out for safety. Later, a rat called Uyenghen in Bini and ...... in Yoruba began to rejoice for surviving the ordeal by singing; eesemi bona meeku. When Ogun saw them running out, he decided to pursue them to wherever they went. He did not however succeed on that day. Since then, he began to hunt for them and to kill which ever of them he could lay hands on. That is when hunters began to set traps and to use guns, spears, bows and arrows for killing birds and animals.

When this Odu comes out at Ugbodu therefore, the person will be advised to prepare his own Ogun without any delay and to refrain from holding meetings with people. He should endeavour not to belong to any club or meeting.

He made divinations for the 200 divinities:

Afe fefe fefe,
Ofe ule, ofe ono,
Oun lo nda ifa fun Orunmila,
Abufun ajugo otun,
 pelu ajugo osi,
Nijo tiwon tikole orun,
Bowa si kole aye.

He made divination for Orunmila and all the 200 divinities when they were coming to the world. He advised them to make sacrifice in order to avoid the risk of spending all their time in the forest. They were told to make sacrifice with a he-goat to Esu and that whenever it was threatening to rain, they should continue non-stop on their journey without seeking shelter on the way. Orunmila was the only divinity who made the sacrifice. They subsequently set out for the earth, at the instance of God.

On account of the sacrifice which they did not make, Esu proceeded to wait for them at the boundary between heaven and earth. As soon as Esu sighted them in the distances, the unplugged the rain taps of heaven and it started raining. The rain was so heavy that each of the divinities began to take shelter at various points on their route in the hope of waiting for the rain to stop. Orunmila stopped for a brief rest in the home of Eegun (Egungun) who gave him considerable hospitality. Egungun persuaded him to stay for the rain to stop, but Orunmila insisted on proceeding on his journey. Egungun however gave him a cap to cover his head from the rain and with that he continued on his journey while the others preferred to remain under shelter until the rain abated.

Orunmila received a tumultuous welcome from his children and adherents who had been expecting his arrival. His children gave him new clothes to wear since he was totally drenched. While he was settling down on earth, the others were still hibernating at various points on the route because the rain continued non-stop for three years.

When the rain eventually stopped, Ogun decided that there was no point in continuing on his journey because he was quite happy in his ramshackled abode by the way side. The others also took similar decisions. When Orunmila was asked for the whereabouts of his colleagues, he replied that they had taken shelter from the rain at various points on the way to the earth. That is why to this day, food is given to all the other divinities outside the house, at bush paths and by-ways, away from the house. That is also why Orunmila is the only divinity that is normally served at home.

When this Odu comes out at Ugbodu, the person is advised that when it rains anywhere away from his home or during a journey, he should, never take shelter but make straight for his home in order to enjoy lasting peace and Prosperity.

Oyeku-bi-wori's preparation for his trip to the earth: He made divination for Otiton or Otiku (Refuse-dump)

The last preparation he made before leaving heaven was to offer homage to Olokun with a cock, pigeon, white kolanut, chalk and parrots' feather. He also Paid tribute to God to obtain divine blessing. He finally offered rabbit, seven eggs, a hen, white, red and black cloth to the elders of the night in addition to a he-goat for Esu.

Olokun assured Otiton that he would be served by all divinities and humanity alike. He would never be in want but that he should not forget him, Olokun. He promised Olokun eternal gratitude. When Otiton got to the world, his life was virtually empty, but on account of the elaborate sacrifices he made in heaven, all the divinities and the inhabitants of the earth began to send food, clothes and all items to him. That is why there is no household on earth which does not send food everyday to the refuse-dump.

The most important Ono-Ifa or Odiha which should be made when this Odu comes out at Ugbodu, is to repeat the elaborate sacrifices which Otiton made in heaven so that the person would constantly receive help from all and sundry. If it comes out at ordinary divination, the person will be told to make sacrifice so that he will always receive help from others. He should be told that food and the means of buying it will always meet him at home.

He made divination for Olaleye:

Olaleye was a well-to-do man but unfortunately he had no children. He had several wives but none of them could bring forth a child. One day, his wives threatened that they were going to leave his house, to find salvation else-where. The prospect of living without his wives scared him so much that he decided to leave for the forest to commit suicide. As he entered the bush, he began to cry that he left heaven wishing to have all the good things of life, but apparently his desire for children did not manifest. He was then crying to his guardian angel that he was returning to heaven to make fresh wishes to have children. He cried the song right up to the bank of the river into which he proposed to dive and drown to end his life.

When he got to the river, as he made his last wish still crying, he heard a voice which advised him that he was not destined to be childless. The voice ordered him to return home to look for a visiting awo called Oyeku-bi-wori. After hesitating for a little while, he sat down not knowing what to do next. Before he left the river he heard a thunderous voice telling him that he would have 18 children and that each of his wives would have children provided he followed the advice of Oyeku-bi-wori, babalawo Olaleye tounle shawo lode Igboti. Olaleye lived in the town of Igboti.

On getting home, he narrated his experience to the Oba of the town, who at that time had a visitor to his court. After hearing Olaleye out, the Oba asked him where he was supposed to come across his awo and Olaleye replied that he did not have the slightest clue. At that point the visitor asked him to repeat the name of the awo he was supposed to look for. He replied, that the name sounded like Oyeku-bi-wori. The Awo then brought out his Okpelle to make divination on the veracity of Olaleye's story. It was Oyeku-bi-wori that appeared at divination. At that point, the visiting awo identified himself as Oyeku-bi-wori and that since his own Odu was the one which also appeared at divination, he confirmed that Olaleye's story was not only correct, but also that his cry for children would turn to glory and that the name of his first child should be Ekundayo (meaning, "weeping has given rise to happiness).

The awo then asked him whether he had six wives and he answered affirmatively. The awo then told him to make sacrifice with plenty of ekuru, plenty of eko, 18 rabbits, 18 snails, 18 bats, 18 cowries, eighteen bags of money and plenty of esho eni, the materials used for weaving mats. He was to scatter the seeds of the "esho eni", into the bush. He went home to prepare for the sacrifice. After making the sacrifice, all his six wives became pregnant the following month and they put to bed subsequently after Oyeku-bi-wori had left for Ife, from where he came. Before his wives delivered, the seeds he scattered in the forest had become a huge plantation which is why the first mat prepared in Yoruba land came from the town of Igboti. From using the Esho eni to prepare mats for sale, the family of Olaleye became exceedingly wealthy. He had eighteen children on the whole and did not lack the means of feeding them.

When this Odu comes out at divination, for a person who has long been anxious to have children, he should be told that his problems would soon be over, provided he makes sacrifice. He should be told to name his first child, Ekundayo or his language equivalent of "Weeping has turned to joy". He should make a feast with plenty of Eko and Ekuru.

Chapter 4

OYEKU-SI-IDI

```
I   II
II  II
II  II
I   II
```

Oyeku Kepdi was a very popular Ifa priest in heaven. He performed many remarkable feats, which have remained universal landmarks, both in heaven and on earth.

He made divination for the morning and for the Evening when they were coming to the world:

He made divination for Morning (Aaro) and the Evening (Oju Ale) with the following poem:-

        Ifa Oyeku sidi,
        Idin mon ojo,
        Koni abebe,
        Iyeri ye la bibe
        Sugbon komo,
        Ese ijo gbigbe.

Meaning:-   The worm knows,
        How to dance,
        But has no limbs,
        Its ankle veins can tune,
        Its inner legs to dance,
        Though lacking the strength,
        To lift the legs.

Oju ale (Evening) was told to make sacrifice with snails, sheer-butter (Ori-oyo), pigeon, white chalk, camwood (Osun) in Yoruba, honey and salt, and he made it. Aaro (Morning) on the other hand was told to make sacrifice with honey and snails. He declined to do the sacrifice because it was not elaborate enough. On the other hand, he told the Awo to prescribe the requisite sacrifice for him to make in order to get to the world before Evening. He was not concerned with lasting prosperity in the world for which he was to make the simple sacrifice with snails and honey, but which he refused to do. Since he was in a hurry to reach the world before Evening, he was told to make sacrifice with a matchet, red cloth, palm kernels and a ram. He made the sacrifice and the Awo also prepared Ifa for him. Thereafter he raced to the world, beating Evening who was still looking for money to fund his sacrifice.

Immediately Morning got to the world, all the good things and people of the world embraced him. When Esu was told that Morning did not make sacrifice for enduring prosperity, he raced to heaven to invite the sun to appear because Morning was stealing the show on earth. The sun instantly appeared on the horizon and its rays began to heat up the atmosphere. Before noon therefore, the fortunes of the Morning had begun to flag. The cool air of the Morning had given way to the intense heat of the Sun and people began to take shelter. Morning, had paled into insignificance. The intensity of the Afternoon had driven the cool air of the Morning into oblivion.

That was when Evening arrived on earth, the fortune which the Afternoon seized from the Morning were all transferred to the Evening. Gradually, the Sun began to set and Evening began to flourish. Evening became very cool, prosperous and wealthy.

That is why to this day, the fortunes of the Morning are shortlived. It only lasts from 6 a.m. to 9 a.m. before the Sun appears. He begins to run into difficulties from about 9 a.m. until his fortunes extinguish completely at mid-day. In other words, his prosperity lasts for only three out of a whole day of twenty-four hours. The Evening on the other hand lasts from about 4 p.m., when he got to the prescinct of the earth and began to flourish gradually from about 6 p.m. to the following day.

That explains why those who come into great wealth and prosperity very early in life, either lose everything or die before middle age. That is also why people who are destined to enjoy enduring prosperity have rough times in the morning, work hard in the afternoon and enjoy prosperous and wealthy evenings. It is those who are destined to become wealthy and famous later in life, that suffer hardships early in life. It also explains why generally, those who make it between morning and afternoon often pray to the Almighty God for their prosperity to last through the evening of their lives. In some cultures, children born in the evening are regarded as being senior to those born in the morning of the same day. People not only pray to live long enough to see their children thrive and flourish but also for their children to bury them in the evening of their lives.

That is why Ifa priests have coined the poem as follows:

                Aro mi ire - o,
                Oju ale la ntoro,
                Bi ale mi baa dara,
                Emi yio dupe l'owo Ifa,
Meaning:-   If my morning is good,
                I pray for the prosperity,
                Of my evening to endure,
      To enable me thank Orunmila.

When this ODU comes out at Ugbodu the person should be told to make sacrifice for a prosperous evening and never to be in a hurry to acquire the good things of life.

At divination, the person should be told if already wealthy and young to make sacrifice so that his prosperity might not be shortlived. He should take life at an easier pace.

He also made divination for Agbaa or Ighede (Big Drum) before leaving heaven:

When Agbaa was coming to the world he went to Oyeku-si-di for medicine and charms in order to command honour and dignity on earth. Orunmila told him that he knew no medicines and charms for his purpose, but that if he was interested, he would make divination to tell him the relevant sacrifice to make before leaving for earth. He agreed to do divination at which he was told to make sacrifice, with 201 arrows, a long cane, and 2 cudgels. He was told that he was one of three brothers born of the same mother, but that he was not to tell any of his brothers about the sacrifice he was going to make lest it would not manifest. The names of his other two brothers in order of seniority were the Gong (Gongon in Yoruba and Egogo in Bini) and Maracas (Akese in Yoruba and Ukuse in Bini).

After producing the materials for the sacrifice, Orunmila used a cane to tie each of the 201 arrows round his head, fastening them in place. While he was waiting in Orunmila's house for the operation to be completed, his two brothers were searching for him to eliminate him. When they were told that he was in Orunmila's house, they went to meet him there. When they saw him with his head tied-up, they asked him why his head was fastened and he replied that he was doing so at the instance of Orunmila. The gong took two of the cudgels and began to knock Agbaa on his head. He then began to cry:-

 Mogbo moru,
 Moti she bo,
 Oyeku-si-di.

Meaning:- I have made the sacrifice prescribed by Oyeku-si-di. His cry sounded melodious and that is the sound of the big drum to this day. On the other hand the Gong began to jibe at Agbaa that he was reacting painfully to his beating;

 Araa kan Agbaa,
 Gogogogo,
 Araa kan Agbaa,
 Araa kan Agbaa,
 Gogogogo.

which is also the sound made by the gong when being beaten with a cudgel. On his part, the Maracas said while clapping his hands that the beating of Agbaa only made him to sit down properly by saying:-

 Okpaa keshe keshe,
 Agbaa keshe keshe.

which also corresponds to the sound made by the Maracas to this day.

Meanwhile, however, Orunmila appealed for a cease fire and when they stopped fighting, he told them that the sound coming from their combat was so melodious that it was better for the three brothers to co-operate conciliatorily instead of combating confrontationally. Orunmila then proclaimed with his instrument of Authority (Ase) that from that day, the three brothers would become indispensable to mankind and that whenever the three of them co-operated to act simultaneously, it would be a sign that something pleasant or festive was happening. In their new spirit of reconciliation, Orunmila told them to serve their heads together with a cock. They did the sacrifice and then left for the world, where they operate successfully as a musical trio. That is why to this day, the sound of the Drum, the Gong and the Maracas (notwithstanding the improvement created by modern technology) acting in concert, produce such melodious music that brings joy and happiness to everyone.

When this Odu appears at Ugbodu, the person should be told that his mother has three children and that each of them would be famous, but that their fame would be even more resounding if they agreed to co-operate. He should be advised to make sacrifice with a ram, 16 snails and 2 pigeons to Ifa before he completes his Ifa initiation ceremony.

At ordinary divination the person should be told to serve Esu with a he-goat to avoid the risk of giving away his honour and popularity to someone else.

He made divination for the Snake:

The snake was originally an ordinary rope when he was in heaven. He could neither bite nor harm. He was only used as an instrument for tying loads. When he decided to come to the world, he went to Orunmila for divination. Orunmila asked one of his followers called:

    (Agbaa nimoju,
     Oron tekpe,
     Oun ni ondifa fun ejo)

to make divination for him. The snake was at that time called Alele, which meant the king of ropes. On account of the fact that he was commonly used for tying firewood, both himself and his children had no peace whatsoever. He wanted to be more respectably treated on earth and to have peace and honour.

At divination, he was told to serve his head with white and red kolanuts inside his house, after which he was also to serve his head with another set of white and red kolanuts by the side of the road outside his house in order to command honour, fear and dignity from the people of the world.

After serving his head in the house at night, he left the following morning for the road leading to the venue of the divine council of heaven. He sat down by the roadside to pray to his head. At the same time, God was on his way to the meeting of the divine council. God met Alele praying. When God heard what he was wishing for, He asked Alele to give Him the two kolanuts with which he had been praying. Alele refused to surrender the kolanuts on the ground that he was advised by Orunmila to use them to serve his head. God asked him the desires for which he was serving his head, and Alele replied that he was created as a nonentity and as a universal servant and that he did not want to suffer the same fate on earth, for which he was leaving presently.

Once again, the Almighty father asked him to surrender the kolanuts and he willingly did so. Thereafter, God ordered him to open his mouth. As soon as he obeyed the command, God spoke and spat into his mouth, and without saying any other word, proceeded on His divine journey, while Alele left for his own house. The words which God spoke into his mouth were:-

    Iwo Okun,
    Emi fun o ni ase wipe,
    Oun-ki-oun ti o ba so ni aiye,
    Ni won yi o gbo ni,
    Oke Orun ni ojo na.
Meaning:- You rope, I endow you,
    With such authority,
    That whenever you speak on earth,
    Your words will be heard,
    In heaven on the same day.

That command of God was a metaphor which means that whenever the snake bites, the victim will feel it instantly and if not treated, will get to heaven on the same day.

Alele left for earth the following day. He got to the earth and continued to be used as a rope. Meanwhile, Olofin made divination in his palace and he was advised to make sacrifice to avoid the danger of losing a human soul before the end of that year. He was asked to give a he-goat to Esu in order to have the necessary peace and tranquility to perform his annual festival without losing a soul. He regarded the prediction as far-fetched and so ignored the advice and the sacrifice.

Meanwhile the members of Olofin's household began to make preparations for the annual festival. The Oba's favourite wife led a team to the forest to fetch firewood for use during the festival. After fetching the firewood, they proceeded to procure the ropes for tying them up. The favourite wife of the Oba then saw Alele with its smooth body. After uprooting it from the ground, the rope warned her not to treat him shabbily. She ignored the warning and continued to fold-up the rope. As she folded the rope up to her hands, he attacked her with the help of his newly acquired authority from God. She quickly threw away the rope and shouted for help. All her mates came to meet her. She began to bleed from the point of impact and to vomit. The others quickly rushed her home. But before they got home, she died.

That incident put a stop order on the preparations for the festival. The Oba ordered the royal herald to announce the cancellation of that year's festival. The Oba also decreed that Ejo (as he came to be called thenceforth) or Alele had acquired the instrument of authority (ASE) for respect and honour. The proclamation was made in the following words:

    Keni keni maamu,
    Kpakun Ejo digi loko,
    Ori Ejo Maakpaa irele ejo.

When this Odu appears at divination, the person should be told to make sacrifice to his head with kolanuts at home and outside his house, because he lacks honour and respect. After the sacrifice, he will command respect, fear and recognition among his llow men.

He made divination for the Flesh when he was coming to the world:
When the Flesh was leaving heaven for the earth, he was told to make sacrifice to Esu, Ogun and the elders of the night, and to use a cock and kolanut to revoke the curse of God on him, that since he was made from the sand of the earth, he would end up returning to the sand of the earth. He refused to do any of the sacrifices.

On his way to the earth, he was accosted by Esu who reminded him of the sacrifice he was advised to make to him, but he brushed Esu aside and continued on his journey. Next, he met the divinity of the night who he also ignored. Finally, he met the worm who asked him where he was bound for. He also ignored the worm. The worm then cursed him that for ignoring him, he would forever constitute the food for feeding him and his children. That is why when any person or animal dies, it is the worms that inherit the flesh of their body. That is also how the curse of God on the human flesh has remained unrevoked to this day; "that from the sand you came and to the sand you shall return".

When this Odu comes out at Ugbodu, the person should make a special sacrifice with antelope, bush goat (Edu in Yoruba and Oguonziran in Bini) plantain, 9 snails and a hen in order to live long in the world. He should forbid all the materials mentioned above in addition to refraining from marrying or having any sensual relationship with a widow.

At divination, the person should be told to serve Ogun with a cock and to give a he-goat to Esu to avoid the unpleasant consequences of offending people who are stronger and more powerful than himself. He should have his own Ifa, but if it is for a woman, she should be advised to marry a man who has Ifa.

Chapter 5

UYEKU-OBARA

OYEKU-KPALABA
```
I    II
II   II
II   II
II   II
```

This Odu did not practise much of Ifa art on earth. What is known about him only relates to his Ifa practice in heaven where he made divination mainly for the animal kindred.

His first work in heaven:
   Ifa Oyeku kpa alaba,
   Oyeku kpa bala Ikpabu,
   Babalawo ejo,
   Adifa fun ejo,
   Abufun eye,
   Atunbufun eku,
   Kpelu ihorobi.

He made divination for the snake, birds, rats, cows and ijanikpere when they were all barren. Each of them was advised to make sacrifice in order to have children. Only Ihorobi could afford the cost of making the sacrifice. First, she gave money to the rat to buy her the materials for the sacrifice. The rat bought the materials but used them to make her own sacrifice. She next sent the bird who also diverted the materials for her own sacrifice. Next, she sent the cow and the snake and they treated her the same way by using the materials they bought for her to perform their own sacrifices.

The four of them soon began to have children, they started making jest of Ihorobi, that she was so stupid to have provided money for the rest of them to make sacrifice for themselves, without lifting up herself to solve her own problems. Ihorobi then cried to Orunmila and reported how she was cheated. Orunmila advised her to produce a feather, yellow yam, white yam and a double bladed knife with the appropriate leaves. Orunmila cooked the yams and gave her the knife with which to eat it. She was told that her children would be born with swords in their mouths and that her children would be more powerful than those of the dour sisters who cheated her. She was however warned not to reveal the secret to her children. She later gave birth to 1,000 children. When they grew up, they asked their mother how they came to have swords in their mouths. Their mother refused to disclose the secret to them. As they grew older and stronger, they continued to insist on knowing the reason why they were differently created. Finally, their mother told them that it was because of the dishonesty of her four sisters, the rat, the bird, the snake and the cow.

From then on, the children of Ihorobi began to kill and feed on the children of their aunts. That is why Ijanikpere kills and feeds on all infant animals to this day.

When this Odu appears at Ugbodu, the person should be advised never to send others to do on his or her behalf any task which is fundamental to his or her life. He or she should endeavour to do them by him\her-self to avoid being cheated. His problems, especially of childlessness were caused by members of his family. He should not seek vengeance because his difficulties would abate and he would overcome his enemies.

At divination, the person should be told that he has several enemies creating problems for him in his family. He should have his own Ifa who will end his problems and make him triumph over his enemies.

He made divination for the Horse when coming to the world:

The Horse had made sacrifice in heaven to have children on earth but failed to make sacrifice against the danger of backing other people's children other than her own.

When the Horse grew up, she decided to travel to Oyo. Oyeku Kpalaba told her at divination to make sacrifice with a rat, fish, he-goat, snail and cudgel. She refused to do the sacrifice. When she got to Oyo, people began to ride on her back but she refused to move. Esu then intervened and told them to use a cudgel to beat her for failing to make sacrifice. When they used the cudgel to whip her, she began to move. That was the beginning of how the horse came to be used as a beast of human burden and why it is the only animal so used.

At divination therefore, the person should be advised to make sacrifice to avoid being used as a beast of burden by others and to avoid carrying other people's problems.

He made divination for the Tortoise:

Traditionally, the tortoise only made divination in order to know the direction to which the wind is blowing and not with a view to making the prescribed sacrifice. He prefers to rely on his wits and cunning disposition. He was himself a traditional diviner. On one occasion, as he was preparing to travel out for his practice, he went to Oyeku Kpalaba for divination. He was told to make sacrifice to Esu, his head and Ogun to avoid being caught in his own tricks. He did not do any of the prescribed sacrifices. He then proceeded on his journey. None of the works he did manifested. To avoid returning home empty-handed, he decided to pose as a royal messenger from the Oba of his town. He was elaborately entertained and got plenty of gifts as royal messengers are wont to have.

However, on the eve of his departure, the bona-fide royal messengers from the king landed in the town. When they were told that one of their colleagues had been in the town for over a week, they were eager to establish his identity. When they discovered that he was an impersonator, the head of the royal delegation tried the Tortoise summarily and sentenced him to death. He was instantly executed.

When it comes out at divination therefore, the person should be advised not to impersonate without making sacrifice.

Oyeku-Obara's works on earth:

He was a very pugnacious Ifa priest who was often fighting anyone that crossed his path. One day, he decided to go and fight in the land of Ogun. When he consulted Ifa before going, he was advised not to proceed on the journey without serving his head and Esu. He did not consider it necessary to make any sacrifice since no combat had previously defied his fighting ability.

He arrived in the town at a time of total pandemonium. When he enquired about the cause of the commotion, he was told that someone had just been murdered in the town. He immediately went to hide by the side of a palm tree. He removed his Ikin from his waist and enquired what he was to do in the circumstance. His own Odu, Ifa Oyeku Kpalaba, appeared. He was told to go and hide inside a hole because the side of a palm tree could not provide adequate security.

He accordingly entered a concealed hole where unknown to him, there was a Boa. He sat down on the head of the Boa who instantly complained that it was the battle that drove him into the hole and wondered who it was that dared to sit on his head. He replied that he came to take refuge inside the hole, because the people of the town were looking for a stranger who had just entered their domain. The Boa told him that the people were so vigilant that he was sure that they would soon be looking for the two of them inside the hole. Not long afterwards, they saw smoke oozing into the hole. The smoke soon drove out Oyeku-kpalaba from the hole, but the boa said he would not leave the hole because a snake never dies in the hole. He then dug up a hole inside the hole and hid his head inside it for protection against the smoke.

As Oyeku-kpalaba was stepping out of the hole, he was apprehended. He however warned them not to arrest, molest or kill him because he was an Ifa Priest. It is commonly known that it is forbidden to arrest, manhandle or jail an Ifa priest. His captors however insisted on taking him to the Oba's palace. When the Oba asked him to identify himself, he again disclosed that he was an Ifa priest and that his name was Oyeku-kpo-bara. The Oba then ordered that a house should be prepared for him and that he should be persuaded to disclose what he came to do in the town. He subsequently revealed that he came to fight with Ogun. He was however told that that was not Ogun's town but the town of Uja, the wife of Ogun, who is the force and power behind him. The people then prevailed on him to remain in the town to practice Ifa art there.

He prospered in the town, but still did not make the sacrifice to his head and Esu. Meanwhile, he was arranging for a wife to be sent to him from his town, but he was told that it was forbidden to bring a bride into the town unless he went to another town to marry her. When he consulted Ifa, he was reminded of the sacrifices he was earlier told to make. At that point, he served his head with a cock and Esu with a he-goat. He eventually prospered immensely ever after.

When this Odu comes out at Ugbodu, the person should serve his Ifa with another at because of an impending catastrophe. He should also be told that there is a sick person in the house where the Ifa initiation ceremony is taking place and that he or she bound to die. The initiate should be told never to arrange for a wife for anybody cause his Ifa forbids it. At ordinary divination, the person should be told to serve Esu ith a he-goat without any delay to avoid the danger of attack by robbers.

Chapter 6

OYEKU - OKONRON

OYEKU - KPELESEKON

```
II  II
II  II
II  II
 I  II
```

He made divination for Iroko and his two sisters:
It was Oyeku-kpelekon roko who made divination for Iroko and his two sisters when they were coming to the world. Iroko gave a goat to his guardian angel and a he-goat to Esu. Oyeku-kpelekon also made a divination for the mother of laity and the mother of the witches, who had Iroko as their eldest brother. Iroko was a very tall and handsome man. After making the sacrifice, he left for the world, where he preferred to settle down in seclusion away from the town. The mother of the laity was the next to come to the world. She preferred to live among human habitation in the town. She had a total of ten children before her junior sister, the mother of witches came to the world where she decided to stay with the mother of the laity. She had only one child.

One day, the mother of the laity (Ogboi) decided to travel to Oja-ajigbomekan akira, the only market where the inhabitants of heaven and earth commonly traded. It used to take three days to return from the market. As she was leaving for the market, she left her ten children to the care of her sister, the mother of witches (Aje). The latter took great care of her sister's ten children before she returned from the market. The mother of laity was very grateful to her sister for the good care she took of her children.

Not long afterwards, the mother of witches (Aje) decided to travel to the market leaving her only child under the care of her sister. Soon after her departure, the children of the mother of the laity (Ogboi) told their mother that they wanted to eat a bird. Their mother offered to slaughter a fowl for them to eat, but they insisted on having a bird. They had their eyes on the only child of the witch mother (Aje or Azen). Ogboi however decided to go to the forest to look for birds for her children.

As soon as she left for the bush, her children attacked Aje's only child and roasted him up for food. While still on her way to the market, Aje got a foreboding which made her to wonder what was happening at home. As her body sign became persistent, she decided to abandon her trip to the market and to return home. On getting home, she discovered that her only child was missing. Soon afterwards, Ogboi also returned from the bush with some birds for her hungry children. After searching in vain for her dead child, Ogboi narrated how she went to the forest to look for birds in response to her children's desire to eat a bird. It soon became apparent that Ogboi's ten children had eaten up the only child of Aje.

Aje lamented that although she took good care of her sister's ten children when she went to the market, she could not return her good gesture by providing adequate custody for her only child when she left for the market. She decided to pack her belongings from Ogboi's house and left for good, crying her eyes out towards the direction of their brother's (Iroko's) residence. Iroko pacified her by reminding her of the heavenly law which forbade cannibalism, and since Ogboi was the first to strike, she would receive a harder blow in return. Iroko from then on provided accommodation to Aje, proclaiming that all the human and material possessions of Ogboi would live at the mercy of the witch-mother. Aje and Iroko then began to feed on the children of the mother of the laity. Before the break of the next day, the witch mother with the active cooperation of Iroko started plucking the children of Ogboi one after the other. It is that first blow dealt on the witch mother by the laity that we all non-witches are children of the laity-Ogboi, repay to the cult of witchcraft to this day.

After losing about five of her children to her avowed enemies, Ogboi appealed to Orunmila to save her from the wrath of her sister and brother. Orunmila reminded her of the sacrifice she failed to make before leaving heaven. She finally made the sacrifices, one with a he-goat to Esu and the other which was taken to Iroko's house to atone for her negligence. When she got to Iroko's house, she surrendered the goat. When her sister, the witch mother wanted to attack her, their brother Iroko intervened. That is the debt we re-pay to witches to save our lives and those of our children through sacrifice to the night, to this day.

When this Odu comes out at divination, the person should be told that he or she is having problems from close relations arising from a bad turn he or she initiated. He/she should make sacrifice to atone for it. If it is Ayeo, he should serve Esu with a he-goat and the Night through Ifa with a hen or a rabbit. If it is Uree he should be told to serve Esu with a chicken and the Night with a rabbit to avoid the risk of offending someone much stronger than himself.

He made divination for Orunmila during a contest over a dead Elephant

Erin ku sinu oko, Odija agba meji:

An elephant was shot in the forest and it came to die at the entrance to the town. When it fell to the ground, its feet pointed at the direction of Alara's house and the head pointed to the direction of Orunmila's house. Orunmila and Alara both claimed ownership. Their conflicting claims gave rise to a dispute which was remitted for settlement to Olofin.

Orunmila made divination and he was advised to make sacrifice with a bunch of palm fruits. Meanwhile, Olofin told them to return home and to report back to the palace later. That gave Orunmila the chance to make the sacrifice.

Next day, they returned to Olofin's palace. Olofin asked each of them to state what they used to cook the poison that killed the elephant. Alara replied that he used the red feather of a parrot, Aluko, and aligator pepper to prepare the poison. On his part, Orunmila reported that he used a bunch of palm fruits to prepare the poison. Olofin then ordered that the elephant should be butchered to determine the ingredients for the poison that killed it.

When the elephant was butchered they saw particles of palm fruits all over its body. Olofin then decided that the elephant belonged to Orunmila.

When it comes out at divination in respect of a contest, the person should be told to make sacrifice to Esu with palm fruits in order to win the contest.

He made divination for Baba Oke Odo to become rich:

Baba Oke Odo was a very poor farmer who had been working hard on his farm but was receiving inadequate reward for his efforts. He then went to Orunmila for divination. He was told to make sacrifice with 4 hens and 4 pigeons because he was going to become rich within three months.

Meanwhile, he set about his farm chores. After felling the trees, firing the farm and clearing the stumps, it was time to cultivate the yams. As he was digging the ridges for planting the yams, his hoe struck an object which turned out to be a pot of treasure hitherto concealed beneath the earth. The contents of the pot when exhumed turned out to be priceless treasures which transformed him into a wealthy man. He subsequently went to thank Orunmila.

When this Odu comes out at divination for a person who is crying for wealth, he should be told that his prosperity is close at hand, provided he makes sacrifice.

He made divination for Elekan:

Elekan had been suffering from the evil machinations of mankind. He eventually went for divination to find out what to do in order to triumph over his enemies.

> Oyeku kpelekon,
> Osho awo ilu igbo,
> Aje awo-oye iyara.

He was told to make sacrifice with a he-goat to Esu and he did it. After the sacrifice, three of his worst enemies committed a capital offence by using a newly born child to make medicine to kill him. When they were subsequently arrested they confessed to the charge and named four other enemies of Elekan. The three capital offenders were executed and the four others were banished from the town into exile. That was how Elekan triumphed over his enemies. He led a peaceful life thereafter.

At divination, the person should be told that he has seven bitter enemies, three of whom are preparing medicine to kill him while the other four are worrying him through witchcraft. If he makes sacrifice he will out-live them.

Orunmila's special punishment for any wife who divorces him:

He made divination for Ojiji when she was going to marry Igun-nigun. She refused to make sacrifice because she rejected Igun-nigun as a husband on the ground of his bald headedness. While still refusing to make sacrifice, she was again betrothed to Akalamaigbo, who she also turned down on the ground of his broad chest.

She was eventually given in marriage to Orunmila, who she again rejected because of his dark complexion which she likened to black soap. As she was leaving Orunmila's house, he stretched out his divination wand and cursed that never again would she know any sleep, because the male duck or drake does not sleep. That is why the shadow does not sleep. Orunmila prepared a special sacrifice with parts of a broom tied up with black and white thread, and kept it dangling on his Ifa shrine. He kept it on his shrine very early in the morning with the incantation that the woman will neither sleep in the afternoon nor in the night. This is the medicinal preparation which Orunmila uses to punish any woman who leaves him unjustifiably. If eventually the woman comes to ask for forgiveness, the preparation is removed from the Ifa shrine and placed in a gutter on which water flows, adding sheer-butter (ori-oyo) and palm oil. Thereafter the woman will stop suffering from insomnia.

He made divination for three brothers — all fishermen:

There were three brothers who in order of seniority were respectively called: Olikatirege, Oligbonjamuko and Elesetirege. They were in the business of isolating a portion of the river, bailing out the water and collecting the fish, that is, pond fishing, (Obu in Yoruba).

One day, as the senior brother Olikatirege was bailing water out of their portion, he fractured his hand. When the second brother Oligbonjamuko was shouting, he broke his jaw. When Elesetirege the most junior discovered the plight of his two elder brothers, he decided to run home for help. As he was running home, a rope twisted his foot and he fell down, breaking his legs.

When Okere (Squirrel) saw him falling to the ground, he began to laugh hilariously. The boa (Oka or Arunmwoto) who by tradition runs for dear life as soon as the squirrel starts laughing, started running helter-skelter. He ended up running into the hole of a rabbit. When the rabbit saw the boa, she realised that the same hole could not contain the two of them without fatal consequences to herself. The rabbit then ran out of her hole. When the monkey saw the rabbit running in fright, he remembered that the sight of the rabbit in broad day-light invariably meant calamity. He then climbed far up on the oak tree. When the monkey finally settled down on one of the branches of the oak tree, the tree warned him that the branch on which he was standing had been paining him for the last three years. The monkey ignored the warning. On the contrary, he began to pace up and down on the invalid branch of the oak tree. Soon afterwards, the branch broke and it fell on the stack of 201 eggs which the guinea-fowl had laid at the foot of the oak tree. When the guinea-fowl returned to her roost, she discovered the tragedy that had befallen her. She began to yell and scream with the words:

Ara kan mi go-go-go-go.

Elegbede (Gorilla) who was in the vicinity overheard the cry of the guinea fowl which was a signal that war was at hand. In preparation for the expected combat, he began to beat the drum on his chest; gidi-gidi-gidi-gidi. The beating of the Gorilla's drum startled the elephant who thought that war had broken out. The elephant started running aimlessly, until he ran into the town. When the cow and other domestic quadrupeds saw the unusual sight of an elephant in the town, they too began to run for their lives. The Oba of the town had one eye and one child. As the cow was running he treaded on the only child of the Oba and he died instantly.

The wife of the Oba (Olori) quickly ran into the room to alert the Oba about the strange events. She pointed out her fore-finger to ask the Oba whether he did not hear what was happening. AS the Oba got up to rise to the occasion, the sharp nail of the woman's pointed fore-finger pierced deep into his remaining eye and he became totally blind.

In the wake of the total pandemonium, the heavenly messenger appeared from nowhere to order and procure a cease-fire. He assembled all the dramatis personae of the morbid drama to narrate the cause of their diverse problems. The three brothers explained that before leaving for their fish pond, they had been to Orunmila for divination and he had advised them to give a he-goat to Esu, which sacrifice they intended to make upon their return.

The sacrifice was to be made to avoid an imminent catastrophe. The squirrel on the other hand explained that he was just returning from Orunmila who had advised him to give palm fruits to Esu to avoid causing a furore, the enormity of which would have proportions bigger than himself. He was just eating one of the palm fruits he procured from the palm tree when he saw a huge man reeling on the ground and he could not help laughing. The boa on his part, explained that since the hilarious laughter of the squirrel killed his parents and grand-parents, he had developed the habit of running for cover each time he heard the squirrel laughing.

The rabbit averred that since the boa was the bane of his kindred having swallowed his parents and grand parents in years gone by, he had gotten used to the reflex action of running away any time the snake entered his house for any reason whatsoever.

The monkey on his part, explained that since it was axiomatic that the sight of the rabbit running in broad day light spelt ominous danger, he had to run up the oak tree. The oak tree recalled the warning he gave to the monkey that he was menacing his invalid hand and failed to heed his warning before the hand broke. The guinea-fowl complained that the eggs she produced over a span of 201 days perished before she returned home. That was why the sight of the calamity gave her a feat of paranoia. The Gorilla explained that his parents had forewarned him that any time the guinea-fowl rang her bell, he should start drumming on his chest. The elephant also said that experience had taught him that any time the Gorilla beat his drum, it was the sign of a calamitous foreboding which was why he began to run for his life because he knew that the physical manifestation of the danger could affect him.

The Cow explained that since the open township was not the traditional habitat of the elephant, he instantaneously began to run at the sight of the elephant in the course of which he inadvertently trampled on the only son of the Oba. Olori explained that it was the excitement of the death of the only child of the Oba that sent her into 'delirium tremens' in the course of which she unwittingly pierced her finger into the Oba's only eye to make him totally blind.

The adjudicating messenger of God from heaven declared all the others innocent, with the exception of the three pond-fishing brothers and the squirrel who delayed their sacrifices. He then proclaimed the restoration of the status-quo-ante of all the affected victims of the catastrophe. That proclamation restored all the broken hand, jaw and leg of the three brothers, re-established God's earlier decree at the beginning of time that the boa will die the very day he kills the rabbit or any of her children, decreed that never again should the boa enter any hole, restored the 201 eggs of the guinea fowl, the hand of the oak tree, restored the life of the Oba's dead son and his sight, and returned the elephant to the forest forever. The second proclamation of the heavenly messenger was that the squirrel should no longer laugh at anyone he sees from then on, with the exception of the boa who he was traditionally appointed by God to warn others of his presence at any location because of his venomous weapon (Ase) which he was warned not to use arbitrarily.

When this Odu comes out at Ugbodu, the person should be told to make sacrifice because he was destined to be a great man and to do great things, provided he made the requisite sacrifice, failing which he could cause a crisis of abominable proportions in his town or in his family. He should serve Esu with a he-goat, squirrel, boa, the head of a rabbit, the feather of a guinea fowl, the branch of an oak tree, the meat of elephant and bones of domestic animals. This is the special sacrifice he must make before the conclusion of his Ifa initiation ceremony.

At ordinary divination, the person should be told to have his own Ifa without delay. If she is a woman she should be advised to marry an Ifa man. He or she should however make sacrifice with a he-goat and a drum prepared with cocoyam leaves and give a cock to Ogun to avert the danger of becoming the victim of an undeniable falsehood. For a person born of this Odu, he should make special sacrifice with a goat and a hen in order to live long and to avoid doing any harm to others. He should forbid alcohol, roasted yam and the meat of a he-goat. He should also prepare his own Ogun shrine.

Chapter 7

OYEKU — BI IROSUN
OYEKU — GBOSUN

```
I    II
I    II
II   II
II   II
```

He made divination for Eyele and Adaaba:

In heaven, after Eyele (Pigeon) and Adaaba (Dove) decided to come to the world, they went to Oye-ngbosun for divination on what to do to have children on earth.

      Ifa oye ngbosun
      Oju mi to ni nse awe ile,
      Irin ese mi jina ni nse awo iba odán
      Bi oti wu ki irin-ajo jinato,
      Ti o ba pe orun le isan meta
      A-o-rin-rin-rinde be.

These were the Awos who made divination for the Pigeon and the Dove in order to have children on earth. They advised the Pigeon to make sacrifice with Elo Osun (Camwood), corn, a bunch of firewood and unused clay pot. After performing the sacrifice, the Ifa priest told her that the materials used for making the sacrifice would appear as birth-marks on the body of her children. When the Pigeon subsequently had children on earth they began to use sticks for preparing their beds on the inner bottom of a clay pot or its equivalent and the camwood appeared as red marks on the feet of her children.

On her part, the Dove was told to make sacrifice with chalk, a bunch of firewood, guinea corn and all kinds of fruits. After making the sacrifice, the Ifa priest told her that the materials used for the sacrifice would feature on the bodies and behavioural pattern of her children. When she began to have children on earth, they displayed a white chalk round their neck and used pieces of sticks to line their nest.

When the two sisters started having children, they began to sing in praise of Oyeku-bi Irosun, thus; Oye-ngbosun to-to-fun.

When this Odu appears at divination, the person should be told to make sacrifice with white chalk, and camwood as well as Pigeon and Dove. He or she will have a fair complexioned child who will do well enough in life to be able to build his or her own house.

      Oyeku-bi-Irosun leaves for the world:
      Erin ku, omu eyinre gbeke,
      Efon atiku ono wo ro de tan-tan-tan,

were the awos who made divination for this Odu when he was coming to the world. They told him to make sacrifice with; a rabbit to the Night, and a he-goat to Esu in order to obviate the danger of dying by the hands of a woman. He was advised neither to make any wife his favourite, nor to rely too heavily on any woman. He was also warned to avoid swearing not to eat any food. He made all the sacrifices.

When he got to the world, he became a practising Ifa priest and he had many wives. One of his wives was very harsh and temperamental. One day, the cantankerous wife prepared food for him but he did not like the food. He was so disgusted with the behaviour of the woman that he swore never to eat the food, in contravention of the injunction given to him in heaven. Following repeated passionate entreaties made by the woman to him in the night, he agreed to forgive her but told her to prepare another food the following morning. The woman prepared another soup as he directed but washed the meat in the soup which he swore not to eat the previous evening and used them to prepare the new soup. He ate the new soup.

There was one family divinity which Oyeku-bi-Irosun inherited from his father, which he used to serve from time to time. When he got to the shrine of the divinity to serve it on the next occasion, the usual signs of acceptance of worship failed to manifest because he had contravened the oath he swore, not to eat the food prepared by his recalcitrant wife, albeit unknowingly. That is why the divinity also refused the sacrifice he made to it. Meanwhile, things began to get sour for him as a result of which he invited Awos to make divination for him. They told him that he had contravened an injunction by eating a forbidden food. He ruminated at length without being able to place the circumstances in which he ate any forbidden food. To revoke the oath, the Awos told him to produce a rabbit, a hen and his own mud image. However when he got to the shrine of the divinity to serve it, he collapsed and died.

When this Odu comes out at Ugbodu the person should be given the same warning that Oyeku-bi-Irosun was given in heaven. He should be told that if he has cause to reject the food prepared by any of his wives (because he will have more than one wife) he should not allow the offending wife to prepare another food for him for a period of at least seven days. He should invite any of his other wives to prepare food for him. Before the completion of the Ifa initiation ceremony, he should serve the night with a rabbit and Esu with a he-goat. He is likely to have one divinity other than Orunmila which he inherited from his father, he should serve it with a cock and beseach it not to allow him to become the victim of his own oath.

At ordinary divination, the person should be told to
serve the night with a rabbit and Esu with a black hen to avoid the danger of dying by the hands of a woman.

Reason for a short life-span:
Anybody for whom this Odu appears at Ugbodu is bound to be a fae, and unless by the special grace of God and Orunmila through appropriate sacrifice, is not likely to live long on earth. As soon as the Odu appears at Ugbodu, a special sacrifice should be made with a he-goat and a U-belt with which the skull of the he-goat is to be nailed to the shrine

of Esu.

The new Ifa should be given another goat to feast his fellow-faes to get them off his back and a special cudgel should be prepared and be given to Esu with which to drive his cohorts to heaven to leave him to endure on earth. This sacrifice should be made after his next marriage following the completion of the Ifa initiation ceremony. The sacrifice should actually be made at the naming ceremony of the first delivery of the new wife which child will be a boy.

> Oye ngbosun oto lojumi, Oto lo jure,
> Oun lo 'obirin fi gbe eru oja,
> Awon lo 'ndifafun oye ngbosun,
> Nijo toun gbe ojuminto shaya,
> Lo 'nbi omo okunrin ti ankpe Adagba.

They made divination for Oyeku-bi-Irosun when he married a wife called Ojumito who gave birth to a male child called Adagba. They told him to make sacrifice with a goat and a hen to Ifa and a he-goat to Esu. They told him that unless he made the sacrifice the child would live and he would die. The wife however persuaded him to delay the sacrifice until after her post-natal bleeding. He died before the sacrifice could be made. When this Odu appears at divination however the above sacrifice should be made without any delay with the following incantation:

> Adagba mi Irosun,
> Iyomo deje lomo,
> Ruja, iyomo.

This is the song, with which the goat is usually slaughtered for Ifa. The sacrifice is made with both the feet of the goat and a hen. That is the only way to save a fae to live long on earth.

The marital experience of Oyeku-bi-Irosun:

One of the characteristics of this Odu is that his son will always have problems with marriage. Therefore, as soon as he discovers that there is another man seeking the hands of his lover he should surrender the woman to the other man. He is forbidden to contest for a woman's hands in marriage.

His first marriage was riddled with unhappiness. He met the woman and immediately fell head-over-heels in love with her and offered to marry her. However, it was not long before he discovered that another man, who was a trader by profession, was also interested in the same woman. One day, she told the two lovers separately that he was going to perform a special ceremony in three days time and invited both of them to be present.

On the appointed day, the Ifa priest and the trader met at her house. She introduced the two of them, disclosing that they had both been her lover, but that the time was ripe to choose which of them was fit to be her husband. She asked them to declare their credentials. The trader declared that he had plenty of money and that since there was nothing that money could not buy, he was capable of providing optimum satisfaction for her. The Ifa priest on the other hand declared that he was a diviner capable of seeing and disclosing all hidden secrets.

As if to test their aptitudes, she asked the trader to put down any amount he could afford and he put down one thousand bags of money (N500). Knowing that her father was late, she told the Ifa priest/diviner that her father promised to see her that day. She wanted him to confirm whether she would actually see her father that day. After divination, he told her that before she went to sleep on that day, she would actually see her father. She retorted by challenging him that he was incapable of seeing anything because her father had long been dead. Consequently, she dismissed him for incompetence and declared him ineligible for her hands in marriage.

When he got home, he consulted his Ikin to find out why he suffered the disgrace in the hands of his lover. He was advised at once to give a he-goat to Esu, which he did immediately.

Meanwhile, Esu had transfigured into a young and handsome light-complexion man and went to the woman's house where he met her playing Ayo game with her trader-lover. When she saw the irresistibly handsome young man, she instinctively invited him to play Ayo with her. The young man however replied that he was in a hurry to get to the next town. She persuaded him not to leave by asking the trader to leave her place because she had finally seen the man she wanted to marry. The young man however told her not to sack her fiancee because he was not ready to marry. Besides, he tickled her femininity by adding that he was convinced that she was not in a position to have the credentials of a woman fit to be his prospective wife. Asked what the qualifying credentials were, he declared that the woman should be fatherless and be capable of removing the last remaining fruits on top of an apple tree for him. The woman instantly disclosed that she had no father. Since the young man had sighted an apple tree at the entrance to the town the woman pointed at it and agreed to go and pluck its remaining fruit. She immediately climbed the tree, but as she stretched her hand to pluck the apple Esu, blinked his eye to her and she fell down from the top of the tree and died instantly.

As everybody began to reminisce that the Ifa priest did predict that she would see her father presently, the trader-lover went away. Esu went back to alert Oyeku-bi-Irosun that the woman had died. Oyeku-bi-Irosun told Esu that his honour and dignity would not fully manifest until the woman was made to resurrect from her death, so she could narrate how she saw her father and then marry him. Esu advised him to go by himself to revive her since he knew what to do.

Oyeku-bi-Irosun went with his Oroke and met the people making arrangements for her burial. He quickly stopped all the burial arrangement and told them to give him an opportunity to bring her back to life. He told the people to sit her up while he pointed his Oroke at her saying:-

Ahunji, **ahunji, ahunji,**
Baaba sun **sejirin,**
Ahunji, ahunji, ahunji
meaning: Arise, arise, arise,
Wake up from sleep,
'Cause one wakes up after sleeping,
Wake up, wake up, wake up.

Almost instantaneously, she woke up and there was general rejoicing. Oyeku-bi-Irosun asked her whether she saw her father and she replied that she did. She then got up and embraced him, thus declaring him her husband. She became the first wife of Oyeku-bi-Irosun giving birth to three children named: Ifatuga, Ifayemi and Ifawale.

At Ugbodu therefore, the neophyte should be advised not to contest with any man for the hands of a woman. When he starts wooing any woman for marriage he should immediately offer a he-goat to Esu to avoid any embarrassing rivalry. At ordinary divination, the person should be advised to offer a he-goat to Esu to avoid any unwelcome contest over his own rightful asset. He should not abandon anything to anyone in anger or out of surrender because it rightly belongs to him.

Chapter 8
OYEKU — BO — OWANRIN

```
II    II
II    II
I     II
I     II
```

Oyeku-bo-Owanrin made divination in heaven for Afi dudu kpa Oju who was the mother of the Rain.

Ifa Oye Wo-rin-mi, Oye won-rin-mi,
Oye-won-rin-je, Oye-bi-o-bale won rin mi,
Ki o won irin mi.
Bi o ba le won, Irin si 'nu,
Ki o won irin si inu.
A kole tori wi pe o won irin mi,
A kole so wi pe o won irin si inu,
Ki a ma pe o ni eji-oye.

The mother of the Rain was at that time, desperate to have a child. She was advised to make sacrifice with a black sheep, a black garment, plenty of soap, and plenty of cudgels and to give a black he-goat to Esu. After making the sacrifice, she became pregnant. That is why when this Odu appears at Ugbodu, the person should be told to make a similar sacrifice in order to avoid the risk of childlessness.

When she gave birth to a child called Ojo or Rain, her contemporaries ridiculed her for having a charcoal-black child who was thought to be incapable of doing anything tangible. Esu however soon dressed him up with black attire, rubbed his face with the foam of soap, and gave him several cudgels with which to beat anyone who dared to challenge him. By the time the Rain began to demonstrate his prowess, there was total darkness in heaven and people began to wonder what he was up to. The cloud had gathered and the soap foam on his face began to show, as he was using his cudgels to beat all and sundry, friends and foes, old and young, high and low, day and night, trees and animals. The darkness before the rain represents the black dress with which Esu clad him. The whole cloud which clears before the Rain represents the soap foam on his face while the showers of Rain represents the cudgels in his hand with which he beats all and sundry.

It was at that stage that his mother rejoiced that she had afterall given birth to a great child. It is on account of the way people laugh at him that explains why it is said that the rain has no friends and why he beats everybody indiscriminately to this day.

At divination for a woman looking for a child, she should be told to make sacrifice because she would give birth to a child whose fame would be felt throughout the face of the earth and whose greatness would shake the community in which he lives and beyond.

He made divination for Ogun's seven children:
When Ogun was despatching his seven children to the world, he went to Oyeku-bo-Owanrin for divination. He was advised to make sacrifice with 7 cocks and seven kolanuts and to give a he-goat to Esu so that they might never be sick. He made the sacrifice. That is why Ogun is never sick.

At divination for a sick person, he should be told to serve Ogun with a cock and kolanut and to give he-goat to Esu to become well.

He also made divination for the swamp:
The swamp was malignately ill. He was told to make sacrifice with his own black apparel, a pigeon, a snail and a three-piece kolanut. He did not have any faith in the sacrifice because he had been sick for a long time. That is why the swamp (IRA in Yoruba and Ekhuorho in Bini) has remained permanently ill ever since. After suffering feats of epilepsy for a long time, which made him to be falling down on side-ways and by-ways, he sought permanent accommodation with the river on whose periphery he resides to this day.

When this Odu appears at divination, the person should be advised never to live in a house near the bank of a river. Wherever he is living, he should serve Ogun with a cock and Esu with a he-goat at least once a year. He should not eat rabbit, pigeon and melon. He can only succeed in any profession that has to do with engineering. Any other vocation will end up in colossal failure.

The birth of Oyeku-bo-Owanrin:
Oyeku-bo-Owanrin was born to a family at Ilere-Otun which was at war at the time of his birth. The war subsequently sent his mother back to heaven. When he grew up, he began to trade in medicinal articles (Iwoshi woshi in Yoruba and Emwin Kemwin in Bini). He succeeded immensely in the business because he was doing it with the active support of his mother in heaven. He was also a practicing Ifa priest on the side-line.

All the animals of the forest used to hold meetings every five days. At every meeting, each animal was required to feast the others with his mother. When it came to the turn of the antelope to kill his mother to make his feast, he went to Oyeku-bo-Owanrin to purchase the required articles. He wanted to buy the meat of all the parts of the body of an antelope including its head. He was able to buy all the other parts but not the head. He proceeded to use the meat to prepare food for the feast. When the feast was ready, while the meat was being shared, someone observed that the head of antelope's mother was not in the soup. The antelope retorted by challenging everybody to confirm whether there was anyone who had killed his mother previously and shared the mother's head to him. No one accepted the challenge. He said he kept away his mother's head because he had previously not received anybody's mother's skull as a share. It was obvious that he did not wish to kill his mother.

Meanwhile, back in his house, the antelope had two servants who he was not treating well. Among the animals were some who doubted the credibility of the antelope's story about his mother. The fox (Ela in Yoruba and Abon in Bini) decided to go and spy on the antelope in his house. The antelope was not in, but the fox met his servants. When he asked for the whereabouts of the antelope, they told him that he was away to visit his mother. The fox was astonished and he exclaimed ironically whether the antelope was going to visit his mother in heaven. He further asked whether the antelope's mother was still alive and the servants answered that she was very much alive and well. The fox subsequently reported his findings at the next general meeting. The Chairman of the meeting then asked for a volunteer to go and bring the mother of the antelope. The leopard agreed to go. The leopard of course knew where to get her under a particular tree called Omodon in Yoruba or Okhuen in Bini. The leopard met her eating the fallen fruits of the tree. When the leopard gripped her, she appealed to him not to give her away. He hearkened to her appeal but advised her never to come to that tree any longer which advice was to fall on deaf ears because no antelope can ever resist the temptation to eat out of the fruits of that tree. One day, she strode stealthily but irresistably to the foot of the tree and as she was picking the fruits, the hunter took aim and shot her dead. The death of the mother-antelope broke up the meeting of the animals.

When this Odu appears at Ugbodu, the person being initiated should be advised to forbid the meat of antelope and to refrain from joining any meeting as well as engaging in any thrift contribution (Esusu) with other people so that the elders of the night might not have the opportunity of undoing him. At ordinary divination, the person should be advised to have his own Ogun shrine. There is a chieftaincy title in his family which will fall to his turn. He should make sacrifice before taking the title.

He made divination for the town of Ilere-Ude and Ilere-Okun:

The two towns were at war. They invited Oyeku-bo-Owanrin and two other awos to come and make divination for them.

 Oyeku-bo-Owanrin, l'ondifa,
 Gbeni arin Iworiwo gbago,
 Eyi timo ma'she onbe lodo Ikumi,
 Adafafun Onilere-Ude,
 Otu bu owo kan ibo fun won,
 Nilere Okun.

These were the names of the three awos who were invited jointly by the two towns. As they were travelling to Ilere-Ude, they stopped to reason among themselves. One said that on getting to the place, he would proclaim that they could only avoid war by making sacrifice with their sleeping mats. The second one suggested that he would advise them to make sacrifice with their annual masquerade (Egungun) regalias in order to avoid the risk of war. Oyeku-bo-Owanrin however said that his proclamation could only be determined by the outcome of divination. Unknown to them, as they were reasoning among themselves, a palmwine tapper on top of a palm tree saw them and overheard what each of them said. As soon as the three awos left the spot, the palmwine tapper climbed down, took a short cut and made straight for the Oba's palace. He alerted the Oba that he should ignore the prescriptions of the first two awos because they were greedy. He advised that the Oba should only listen to the third one who preferred to base his advice on the outcome of divination. When the three awos eventually landed in the town, they were given a befitting reception and accommodation.

Next morning, they made preparations for divination. When they sounded Ifa with Ikin, Oyeku-bo-Owanrin came out. The first two Awos recommended sacrifice respectively with the sleeping mats and masquerades' regalias of the entire community. The third one, that is the disciple of Orunmila assured them that there would be no more wars provided they could make sacrifice jointly with a goat and to surrender one dark-complexioned spinster in the Oba's household to Orunmila for marriage. That is why when this Odu comes out at divination, the person will be told that he or she was one dark complexioned girl in the house who is destined to be the wife of Orunmila. She will have problems in life unless she is given in marriage to a man having his own Ifa. If she is already betrothed to a prospective husband, the fiance should be advised to have his own Ifa, otherwise, the marriage will not last. By the same token, if this Odu comes out for a man, he should be told to have his own Ifa because he belongs to Orunmila's lineage. He should do so in order to prosper in life.

Meanwhile however, the people made the sacrifice with a goat as prescribed by Orunmila and surrendered the dark complexioned girl. Thereafter the threat of war abated in the two towns.

When this Odu comes out at divination.

The person should be advised not to reveal his plans to anyone and to keep his plans and secrets to himself.

Additionally, the person should be told to make sacrifice with a cock, a hen and all other edible items in order to get all his wishes and desires to materialise.

He made divination for the farmer and his wife:

>Oko ma ke,
>Ale ma sun'kun,
>Olomo ko ni pa omo re je,

meaning:-
>Husband, do not cry,
>Wife do, not lament,
>'Cause a mother does not,
>Feed on its own child.

These were the awos who made divination for Eko, the farmer, and his wife Emelu when the wife was having a secret extra-marital affair. Whenever the farmer went to the farm to harvest and barn his yams, his wife was in the habit of making love on her husband's bed with her lover.

On one such occasion, as they were enjoying themselves on the husband's bed, a pot of melon stored away on the overhead counter in the fire place dropped to the ground and crushed her child who was lying down, to death. When the lover panicked, the unfaithful mother told him not to be unduly disturbed because she could take adequate care of the situation.

She subsequently got up to prepare pounded yam for the husband to eat. When the food was ready, she carried it in a basket on her head to the farm, backing the dead child on her back. On getting to the farm, she hailed on the husband that she had brought food for him to eat. He was busy on the yam barn. The husband invited her to meet him at the barn. She dropped the food inside the hut of the farm and proceeded to meet the husband at the barn. On getting there, the husband told her to lift a tuber of yam for him to barn. She lifted two yams up to him. When the husband took one of the two tubers, she immediately let go the second tuber to fall on her back and it hit the head of the already dead child. She then shouted that the yam had killed her child. The man jumped down in disgust, took the child from her back and observed that its body was already very cold. He wondered why a single yam could have killed the child so instantaneously for the body to have gone so icy-cold. Meanwhile, the mother abandoned the child to his father and cried home. Before she got home, the lover had committed suicide by hanging himself. Eventually, the husband came home with the dead child and made straight for the home of the above-mentioned Ifa priests with the wife accompanying him. After divination they told the wife that she lost the child on account of her unfaithfulness and that she had a wicked mind. She was told that the child did not die in the farm but through the impact of a pot of melon. She was asked to confess to what she was doing when the child died. She broke down to confess when she was told that the other party to whatever she was doing when the child died had already taken his own life and that she would also die ignominiously if she failed to make a clean breast of what happened. At that point she confessed to what actually happened. The husband then began to cry and the awos sang with the signature tune of this Odu.

Oko maake,
Ale maasunkun,
Olomo kiikpa,
Omo reje,
Aini gbagbo,
Lo'nti kpa omore,
Ifa ti so dodo ege,
Oti so dodo ege.

Meaning:- It is no use crying because parents do not kill their children to eat, but Orunmila has revealed that this particular child was lost to the unfaithfulness of its mother.

When this Odu comes out at divination for a misfortune

between a couple, the wife should be told that she is being unfaithful to the husband. If the misfortune has already occurred, she should be told that she is responsible for it because of her cohabitation with another man, that is, if it is ayeo. If on the other hand it is Uree, she should be told to confess her act of infidelity to avoid the loss of a child and her lover. The man should be advised to serve Ogun to obviate the danger of losing his own life through the infidelity of his wife.

Chapter 9

OYEKU-OGUNDA
OYEKU-IJOMODA-YE
OYEKU-D'OJA

```
I    II
I    II
I    II
II   II
```

This is a powerful disciple of Orunmila. He performed several mysterious feats on earth and was so much the quintessence of a proficient Ifa Priest that his fame echoed both in heaven and on earth. He is noted for knowing the secrets of how to save mankind from the cold hands of death.

He made divination for the Tortoise in heaven:

When the tortoise was making arrangement to come to the world, he went to Oyeku-dooja for divination.

        Be'ni oni iri,
        Ola eribe,
        Oron la e mashe tele ri.
meaning:-   Today cannot be,
        Like tomorrow, because,
        We know not today,
        What we are going,
        To do tomorrow.

These were the names of the awos who divined for the tortoise before he left heaven for the world. At divination, Oyeku do'oja came out. He was told to make sacrifice with a he-goat to Esu to avoid being used as a sacrificial victim for solving difficult problems on account of the way he walks. Since he is not given to making sacrifices, the tortoise preferred to rely on his subterfuge rather than make the sacrifice.

On getting to the world, he began to live on his wits. He entered the world with an iron dress which was his house in heaven. When Esu realised that the tortoise refused to give him food, he decided to betray the myth surrounding his iron dress to mankind. Before then, the tortoise was dreaded by animals and human beings alike. Esu went to Ogun to ask him whether he realised that the flesh of the iron clad tortoise was very sweet and delicious. Ogun told Esu to shut-up because all the divinities knew that the tortoise was the favourite policeman of the heavenly household and that it was suicidal for anyone to dare him. Esu also went to Osonyin (Osun) the medicine divinity as well as Ile (Oto) the ground divinity and told them the same thing about the tortoise. All three of them took note of the information given by Esu and were looking for an opportunity to apprehend the tortoise.

Meanwhile, the tortoise had produced several grown-up children who were moving around fearlessly because of the myth of invincibility surrounding them. One day, as Ogun was moving around in the forest, he found the tortoise also hunting for food. He moved to the back of the tortoise and used a sharp cutlass to cut him into two and discovered that in consonance with the advice of Esu, his meat was actually very tasty. When the other two divinities heard that Ogun had successfully dared the tortoise, they too went after his children and also found their meat to be very delicious.

At divination the person should be advised to have his own Ifa and to make sacrifice to Esu from time to time so that the secret of his endurance might not be betrayed. He should avoid the temptation of relying too exclusively on his wits and stratagem because he would have three deadly enemies capable of ending his life unless he seeks solace with Orunmila. He should refrain from eating tortoise but should nonetheless, use it to serve Ogun, the ground, and Osun after having his own Ifa.

He established the first market on earth:

He had been told at divination to make elaborate sacrifice in heaven because he was going to establish a market on earth. For that purpose, he was required to make sacrifice to Esu with 201 he-goats, 201 roasted yams, 201 plantains, 201 corns, 201 akara and 201 eko because Esu was going to be the architect of his success. Esu was so satisfied with the sacrifice that he went to greater lengths than ever before to contrive how to compensate him when he got to earth.

On getting to the world, he began to practise Ifism. Meanwhile, Esu went to him and advised him to gather many people together to pray for them and to make divination for them at nominal fees and that he should develop the practice of doing that every five days. As the people began to get together, they also started buying and selling goods and services from one another. That was how the first market place originated on earth. Before then, the only known market which was commonly traded by divinities and mortals, heaven and earth alike, was Oja-Ajigbomekon Akira, which was established by God Himself.

When this Odu appears at Ugbodu, the person should be told to make a special sacrifice to Esu by procuring one he-goat and one skull of a he-goat breaking it into 200 pieces, cutting a tuber of yam, one plantain, a tuber of cocoyam, etc each into 201 pieces together with 201 seeds of corn, to be buried on the ground of the market place. After doing the sacrifice, he will prosper immensely as a group gatheren.. That is why this Odu is called Oyeku=do=ja.

He made divination for Ajija (Eziza), Sango and Oro:

The divinities of the wind, thunder and secrecy were friends. One day, they decided to test their individual prowess. Sango proclaimed that he only knew how to dance. Eziza said he knew how to change things, whilst Oro said he only knew how to fight.

Meanwhile, the three of them went to the market where they met Eziza's mother selling medicinal articles (Woshi-woshi in Yoruba and Emwinkemwin in Bini). They also met Sango's mother selling palm oil, while Oro's mother was selling water. Not long afterwards, they became hungry and it was time for each of them to put their avowed capabilities to test. They suggested that Eziza should arrange to steal something for them to eat. He quickly transfigured into a gale-force wind which stole water from Oro's mother, oil from Sango's mother and meat from his own mother, albeit without knowing the victims of his theft. When they later gathered to eat what Eziza had stolen, there was a commotion in the market and all their three mothers were complaining that unknown thieves had robbed them of their wares. They decided to go home to alert their children to what had happened to them. Their three children had eaten and were resting at the three road junction. The hunter was the first to appear before them. When he however sensed what the three men were likely to do, he repeated the following incantation:-

 Orita meta, amidi kugu,
 Bebe ona amidi gere gere,
 Misi aladufe.

By the time the hunter got to the road junction, his conjurement had compelled the three men into a deep sleep. After the hunter had passed, they were aroused from their sleep by the cries of their mothers. They did not know one another's mother. Each of them took position at each point of the three roads converging at the junction. As the wailing women approached, Sango apprehended Oro's mother, Oro captured Eziza's mother, whilst Eziza seized Sango's mother. As they wondered whether their captives were not their own mothers, while their mothers were wondering whether their captors were not their own children, Sango's mother hailed on his son by his true name, Aremu Olufiran. With that call, the men released their respective captives. The women narrated how all three of them were robbed in the market of their wares of water, oil and meat. The three sons on realising what had transpired, had looked at one another with amazement and turned to Eziza to query whether his prowess could only manifest by going to steal from their own mothers. He replied that there was no harm done because it was their mother's food they ate.

At that point, the hunter who had since been watching from a hide-out, emerged to adjudicate over the actions of the three men. He decided that from that day, Eziza would only be able to steal from anyone in the forest, whilst Sango should continue with his dancing spree and Oro to disappear into the woods. Sango's mother was annoyed and decided to return to her father's home town of Takpa. Alafin atiba who became the king of Oyo was given to Sango's mother in exchange for Elenkpe Adodo the king of Takpa. Oro was cursed never to have a shrine. The hunter was Ogun himself.

When this Odu comes out at Ugbodu, the person should be told that either his mother has three sons or that she has three sons in a row. The person himself will marry three wives and whether or not the sacrifice is made, he will be the victim of a robbery but it will not be serious if the sacrifice is made with 2 dogs, a ram, a cock and a tortoise. He should have three additional divinities:- one dog to prepare Ogun, one dog for Eziza, a ram to prepare his own Sango, and the tortoise and cock for sacrifice in a three road junction close to his house. At ordinary divination, the person should be advised to serve

Ogun with a cock and Ifa with a ram and a he-goat for Esu to avoid the danger of an imminent robbery.

Oyeku-do'ja is invited to heaven:

Oyeku do'ja had become very prosperous and famous on earth. He had established the first market on earth which was thriving immensely. The news of his success and popularity on earth had reached heaven. At a subsequent meeting of the divine council of God in heaven, it was decided that the time was ripe for him to return to heaven and the divinity of death was instructed to implement the decision. Death despatched two messengers to fetch him from the earth.

Meanwhile on earth, Oyeku-do'ja made his morning divination and his own Odu appeared. He was astonished because it revealed that the messengers of Death were on their way from heaven to take him away from the earth. Ifa however advised him that if he wanted to prolong his stay on earth, he should immediately make the following sacrifices:-

(1) To slaughter two cocks on the shrine of Esu and cook them with a clay pot and without eating out of it, carry it to the road side where he was to;

(2) Prepare fire for cooking a tuber of yam which he was to leave on the spot after cooking it by the road side together with a gourd of drinking water and another gourd of palm wine.

(3) He was to pack in a bag; the Ikin of his Ifa, some of his wearing apparels including a pair of used shoes, hat, and some of his discarded divination materials, and hang it on a fork stick at the same spot on the road side.

He made the sacrifices and carried them to the road leading to the town. As soon as he returned home, Esu went to hide in the bush near the spot containing the sacrifice which Oyeku-do'ja had made.

When the two messengers of Death arrived at the sacrificial spot, they sat down to rest. They were soon attracted by the alluring aroma of the food. Since they were already very hungry, they sat down to help themselves to the food. After eating to their hearts' content, they drank water and wine. That was the point at which Esu emerged fully dressed as a civil policeman (Akoda in Yoruba and Olakpa in Bini). The heavenly messengers were startled by the sight of the strange figure of an earthly policeman.

Esu challenged them to identify themselves and they replied that they were heavenly policemen sent by the divinity of Death to come and bring an Ifa priest called Oyeku-do'ja to heaven. Esu laughed hilariously and exclaimed; "What a co-incidence". He told them that the Ifa priest was himself already aware that they were coming for him and had packed himself ready for the trip. He added that he was infact already on his way to heaven, a fact which Esu substantiated by showing them the bag hanging on the fork-stick containing his personal effects including the Ikin, Okpele, Orofa and Urukere of his Ifa which were all packed for the trip. Esu went on to ask them who consumed the food and drinks Orunmila kept on that spot. They answered that they ate them because they thought they were used for sacrifice. Esu then told them that they were sacrifice indeed because by eating the food, they had absolved Orunmila from the object of their mission. They retorted that it was Orunmila they came to collect and not his food or sacrifice.

At that point, Esu told them that Orunmila was on his way already and that he only went to fetch a few more materials he needed for the trip to heaven, but that since they had meanwhile stolen the food and drinks, he wanted to use for his trip, he would accompany them to give evidence against them in their consequential arraignment for theft at the court of the divinities in heaven. He reminded them of the heavenly law that stealing was a capital punishment which attracted the death penalty. The heavenly messengers were now completely dumbfounded and began to beg Esu for what they were to do to atone for their offence.

In the negotiation that followed, they agreed to leave Orunmila on earth rather than court the risk of being accused of stealing in heaven, under pain or death. when Esu asked them how they proposed to explain their unaccomplished mission to the divine council in heaven, they disclosed that they had contrived the strategy of going to heaven with the remnants of the food prepared by Orunmila together with his personal effects as evidence of the sacrifice he had made to prolong his stay on earth. They revealed that in heaven, the tradition was that as soon as the person slated for death made sacrifice to save his life, he would be spared. With that, they took their leave to return to heaven. Orunmila lived for several decades after that incident.

When this Odu comes out at divination, the person should be warned that death is on his trail and that on that very day of divination, he should make the above-mentioned sacrifice without any delay. If he makes the sacrifice speedily his life will be safe, but he will nonetheless be the victim of a robbery, as the price he has to pay for his life.

It is important to note that as earlier indicated in the first volume of this work, the author saw the practical manifestation of this Odu on the 1st of June 1980.

At a divination exercise, on the 31st of May 1980 this Odu appeared for him and his Ifa priest told him to make the sacrifice immediately. The sacrifice was done on the same night. The following night, on the first of June 1980, his house at the Airport road in Ikeja was attacked by 40 armed robbers and his life was saved in mysterious circumstances by God through Orunmila.

HE MADE DIVINATION FOR THE DOUBTER:

Oju ugu ye fon,
Oti ku leyin
Adifa fun ita
Abufun awi Igbo,
Ebo ija ki ama'ja
Ki ayewa le toro.

Meaning: The face of the vulture bulges forward; And his stomach protrudes backwards. That was the Awo who made divination for Ita, the doubting Thomas or argumentator.

He also made divination for the man who did not listen to advice. They were both told to make sacrifice to avoid quarrel so that their lives might settle and be peaceful. They made sacrifice with a fowl, a pigeon, rat and snails. Thereafter, they were able to live a successful life.

When this Odu comes out at divination, the man should be told that he is very argumentative and that he also has a close relation, friend, wife, son or daughter who is equally indomitable because, the person does not heed advice. If he can identify the person, they should both make sacrifice in order to get along. Otherwise, there is no way that a person who is argumentative can live successfully with an associate who does not listen to advice.

HE MADE DIVINATION FOR A COUPLE:

Okunrun maa mu ohun mi lo so'run
Adifa fun Ikugbola, oko Atawuro mu ola.
Invalid, do not take my medications to heaven.

Meaning:

That was the name of the Ifa priest who made divination for Ikugbola (Uwuigbefe in Bini), the husband of Atawuro mu Ola when he was indisposed. He was told that death was dancing around him and that he should make sacrifice with a sheep, and a pack of fire-wood. The sacrifice was made and the head of the sheep was buried in front of his house. The sacrifice drove death away and he lived in prosperity to a ripe old age.

A divination, the person should be told to make a similar sacrifice in order to live a long and prosperous life.

Orunmila ni Ojo eni da ni eni nla aje.
Orunmila ni ojo eni da; Moni ojo eni da.
Oni ojo ti eni da, 'pe eni ma gbe iyawo.
Orunmila ni ojo eni da, 'pe eni ma bi omo
Oni ojo eni da, mo ni ojo eni da.
Oni ojo ti eni da, pe oun ma ni gbogbe ire,
ni aiye ni o ma ni
Oni ojo eni da; mo ni ojo eni da.
Oyeku do'ja's special sacrifice against untimely death:

O ni ojo ti eni da, 'pe oun yi o ku,
O ni ojo na ni enia ma ku.
A ni Orunmila, ani ohun ahurin ni yen.
Meaning:
Orunmila says, the birth of a person
Marks the beginning of his prosperity.

He will eventually grow up to marry,
And to have children,
And to be endowed with all material wealth.
He will eventually die on the day,
He was destined to die.
This is the philosopy of life.

Orunmila however emphasized that the manifestation of these desires depends on the amount of sacrifice, which should consist of a ram, the tuber of Abirishoko (Olikhoro in Bini), because death does not eat Abirishoko).

Death eats not the tuber of Abirishoko,
The big ram with large horns,
Uses them to ward off;
The onset of Death.

Orunmila, protect me from the wrath of death and direct the feet of prosperity to me. If this ODU appears at Ugbodu, the person should be advised to make sacrifice with a ram to obviate the danger of death to his close relation. He should also be told that a relation of his is sick and sacrifice should be made to prevent him/her from dying.

Chapter 10

OYEKU - OSA
OYEKU - KPOTA

```
II  II
I   II
I   II
I   II
```

Divination for Esu in heaven:

This Odu gives an account of one of the rare instances in which Esu made divination with Orunmila. When Esu concluded his plans for following the divinities to the earth. He went to Orunmila (Okpa re eyi, Okpa roun) who advised him to make sacrifice to his own soul to avoid the danger of experiencing problems bigger than himself. He was to serve his soul with a he-goat. Esu wondered whether there was any force in heaven and on earth bigger than himself. He made a jest of Orunmila and refused to do the sacrifice. Thereafter, he left for the earth with the determination to destroy any divinity or mortal that dared to cross his path. On getting to earth, he established a farm which soon began to yield fruits before anyone else's. On account of the fact that his farm was the first to yield fruits, others began to steal from it. Esu however wondered who it was that had the courage to steal from his own farm. Unknown to him, it was his own primordial counterpart (Onne in Yoruba or Esuamen in Bini) who was stealing from his farm. Onne had several children and he had earlier also been advised to serve Esu with a he-goat. He too refused to make the sacrifice. He was also advised to make the sacrifice to avoid meeting a force mightier than himself. Onne had also boasted that since he was the guarding force behind Esu, he saw no justification for making the sacrifice. Onne was also advised to prepare a feast for little children which he did, while refusing to give a he-goat to Esu.

When Esu discovered the route which the intruder took to steal from his farm, he arranged to set a trap on it. During Onne's next visit to the farm, the trap caught him. When he realised that it was a very strong trap, he decided not to put up any resistance. He remained quietly with the trap.

The following morning, Esu set out to go and watch his trap. When he saw Onne in the trap, he abused him for being the thief that usually stole from his farm. Onne kept quiet because flies were already flying round him. Esu picked up a missile and threw at Onne but the latter pretended to be already dead. When there was no movement, Esu presumed him to be dead. When Esu however moved to bend the bow of the trap in order to remove the victim from it, Onne held on tightly to Esu. Onne got hold of Esu's matchet and threw it away and they got inter-locked with each other. During the ensuing struggle, they uprooted the trap. Onne tried to pull Esu into the water, while Esu tried to push Onne back on the land. After a long struggle, the children to whom Onne had made a feast overheard the groanings, of the Giants and were curious to find out what was happening. When the children eventually saw who was fighting their benefactor, they flew into his (Esu) eyes. As Esu used his hands to push the children away from his eyes, Onne got the opportunity of pulling clear into the depth of the river. He thus escaped the wrath of Esu, who after retrieving his matchet, returned home, dejected.

On getting home, Esu asked his son, Falsehood, to fetch him water to drink. When the son did not show up with the water in time, Esu hit him on the head and the son died instantly. That was the point at which Esu remembered the sacrifice Orunmila advised him to make. Rather belatedly, he finally made the sacrifice.

When this Odu comes out at divination therefore, the person should be advised to make sacrifice with a he-goat to Esu and feast young children with akara or biscuits in order to avoid a head-on collision with a higher authority.

His experience with his aviary:

Oyeku-kpota was a very proud man. He was a farmer and also kept an Aviary where he reared black and white birds. At one stage, he began to observe that each time he went to the farm, leaving the birds in the aviary, he returned to discover that the black birds had killed one of the white birds. When it became a regular feature, he decided to consult his mother on the significance of the strange occurrence. In reply, the mother queried why he decided to choose the hobby of birds-rearing when he did not belong to any nocturnal club. The mother added that a person endowed with his proud disposition could not dabble into such a hobby without adverse consequencies. He stubbornly refused to change his attitude of not joining any subterranean society but decided to embark on the improvisation of administering oaths to the birds in order to stop the black ones from destroying the white birds. In view of the fact that white birds were his lucky signs, the mother advised him that if he was going to administer oaths to the birds, he should look for the tiokam (Ogbigbo in yoruba and Owonwon in Bini) and a hen with which to administer the oath to them on the bare ground, adding palm frond, Ewe-Igbegbe (Ebe Osan in Bini) and Ewetete (Ebitete in Bini). After getting the materials together, he should put all the leaves on top of the palm frond. He finally inserted the meat of the fowl and the tiokam on top of the leaves and called on each of the two birds to take an oath never again to harm each other nor to harm or destroy anyone and anything belonging to him (Orunmila). As they were taking the oath, he was repeating the following incantation: Ajobu jobu afoyele bule, Eni ba da le koye-leye, Ajobu jobu afogbigbo bule, Eni ba dale ko gbigbo gbo, Aje lo ri ewe aasun lori, Imo afi asho la gheren gheren bura.

After completing the oath taking ceremony, he dug the leaves into the ground, to seal the oath with the authority of mother earth. The practical effect of the oath was to stop the black birds which were esoterically stronger than the white birds who were more numerous from destroying the latter. His own mother was infact a witch, which explains why the mother of anybody initiated into this Odu at Ugbodu must also be a witch.

When the Odu therefore appears at Ugbodu, the person should be advised to offer a goat to the elders of the night to stop witches from continuing to spoil his materials and business, as they must surely have been doing before then. He should be told to stop attending all meetings to which he belongs. He should also be advised to deal discreetly with a lame or crippled member of his family. The sacrifice to be made on account of that person should be done with 4 snails, 4 yards of white cloth and 40k while adding the Iyerosun (divination powder) of this Odu.

At ordinary divination, the person should be advised to serve the night with a rabbit and to refrain from attending any meeting so that people might not bear false witness against him.

Orunmila's poem on prosperity:

Agbon Bi Ako, Ago Bi Ako, Ako Gbon gon, Ako oegbele, Ako go-go-go, Ako kogeeregbe, Moni tani ijako, Orunmila ni Agba to ba, fi'ile ara re sile, Toun tele oun Okpe L'eyin, Oun ni nje ako, Moni iwo oshowo Okpe, Mo le mi Oshowo Okpe, A akii showe Okpe, ki eni ma'laya, Aje ni ba ni kpe ni ni aya, A kii showo Okpe k' eni oma bi 'mo Eru ni ba kpe ni ni Eshin, Moni Orunmila, mo ni kiwo gbemi, Orunmila Oni oun gbemi Oni maagun eshin li osan Oni maagun Eniyan li oru, Moni ofe so mi d'aje 'nla, Oni iro ni kii she aje, Oni ti mo ba gun eshin lo s'ile Olofen li osan, Ti mo lo se awo fun, Ti motun bowale, Ti alele ti mofi obinrin mi sun ti'ra, Ti mo mu eka, ti mo fi lu eturukpon, Aye Olufegun Orika Oshe ekewa, ti won fi bi egidi omo; Oni nje mi oti g'eshin l'osan; Mi de ti gun eniyan li oru, Meaning:

The person who can,
Forsake his home,
To serve Orunmila,
Becomes a strong man,

No one trades on the palm tree, Without making money. Money finances marriage, And children are the profits of marriage. The emergence of a child, Necessitates the use of a servant, And the efforts of a servant, Help to fund, the cost of a horse (or a car). I beseach you Orunmila, To lead me through-out my life. In his response:-Orunmila promised perpetual protection, For his honest and faithful followers, Throughout their lives and beyond. You will ride on a horse (or a car) by day, And ride on a human being at night. Again, his followers asked him;-Father are you going to make a witch out of (us?) To which Orunmila answered negatively, Adding that as my faithful follower, You will prosper to the point at which, You will become the royal diviner, Who will make divination and sacrifice, During the day for Olofen, And return home to rest, And in the night, you will have a wife, To sleep with as a bed-mate. She will become pregnant and Bring forth a child, After nine months. That will be the manifestation of prosperity, That is the translation of the metaphor, That you will ride on a horse by day, And ride on a person by night. That is how I will help my followers in their (lives).

That is why when this Odu comes out at divination for anyone who is struggling for existence, he should be advised to have his own Ifa if he does not already have one. If already has his own Ifa, he should be advised to prepare this special sacrifice (Ono-Ifa in yoruba and Odiha in Bini) because Orunmila will pilot him to the path of prosperity. He will prosper to the point of becoming happily married, having children and owning a car.

Divination for a Contest:

Erin oku, omu ori soko. Litede ofi uru soko lomu toyo. Olutede oni kon tede to. Olomu toyo oni keya yodabo. Erin toba wa ni agbe, Oloja meji. Erin ogun nii o.

Meaning:

An elephant died in the forest, and
Its head faced Olutede's farm, while
Its tail pointed to Olomu-toyo's farm.
They began to contest ownership of the dead elephant, and
Both went for divination and sacrifice was recommended.

The one who made sacrifice won the contest. At divination, Olutede was told to make sacrifice with cock, hen, tortoise and snails. On his part, Olomu-toyo was asked to make sacrifice with cock, hen, pigeon and tortoise. Olutede refused to make the sacrifice because of the maxim that he who owns the head of an animal owns the rest of the body. Olomu-toyo however made the sacrifice and when the matter was referred to the king, it was decided in his favour.

When this Odu comes out at divination, the person should be told that he is contesting for a benefit, but that if he makes sacrifices, he will succeed over his opponent.

Incantation:

Orunmila ni ki Oyeku ye-sa-gara, Moni onise rere ni yio ma je; Oni onise re re ni o je fun alara, ni ojo ti yi o gun ori te baba re, Orunmila ni ki Oyeku-ye-sa gara, Moni onise re-re yi oma je onise, rere ni o je fun Ajero ni ojo ti, yi o gun orite baba re.

Orunmila ni ki Oyeku ye sa-gara, Moni onise rere ni yi oma je. Oun nio je fun Orangun ile-ila ni, Ojo ti o gun orite baba re, Orunmila ni ki Oyeku-ye-sa gara, Moni Onise rere ni yi o maje, Oun ni o je fun loja-loja, oun ni oje fun o, ni ala kan esiwu-eme irun nla tia gun ori, egbonre so igba li ojo ti o lo gun ori ite babare. Orunmila ni Akapo; Moni a i fisi; Orunmila ni ope ni segi, Moni ikin owo mi a dayo. **Meaning:**

Orunmila wanted his creator to know that a Messiah,
Shall come and will be told to make sacrifice with pigeon and white fowl.
Orunmila advised Oyeku to make haste,
The Ifa priest say. Oyeku is the hard working type,
He said he worked very hard for Alara,

When he (Alara) was ascending his father's throne. He was also a hard working man for Ajero, when he ascended his his father's throne. He also worked very hard for Head to eat, work, live, feed and procreate, in the house. Home advised man to go to Orunmila, who brought him (Home) to the world, and gave him authority (Ase) to become the custodian of all mankind.

Orunmila advised man to make sacrifice in order to be able to build and live in the House. He made the sacrifice with a sheep and a pig. Thereafter man built the house, and Home asked man what would happen if he left him to travel out and died during the tour. Man replied that his corpse would be brought home for burial. That is why the human corpse is often brought home for burial after death. When man lives far too long away from home, he is often invited to return home.

Chapter 11
OYEKU - ETURA

```
I    II
II   II
I    II
I    II
```

It was this Odu that revealed how Orunmila taught humanity how to serve him and how to offer food to him to provide salvation to people. Let us now examine how to greet Orunmila in the morning which we shall call the morning prayers in Ifism.

Morning Prayers to Orunmila:

Orunmila ajiborisa kpero,
I offer you morning greetings;
In the name of my Odu (name your Odu);
Just as you wake up every morning;
To offer greetings to Olodumare;
The Creator and Father of all existence.
I thank you for bringing me;
To the beginning of another day;
For guarding me through my sleep;
To see this morning and to look forward;
To the chores of another day;
I thank you most especially;
For not allowing me to offend my fellow men:
Throughout yesterday, because you have ordained;
That to serve God, according to the divine laws;
Your children should be able to tell you;
Every morning that they have succeeded;
In resisting the temptations;
To do any wrong against Olodumare;
The two hundred (200) divinities;
All the children of God;
And the society in which they live
Furthermore, in accordance with your injunction;
I have refrained from avenging all wrongs;
Done to me by my relations, friends and foes, and
done good turns to all my friends and enemies alike;
Help me also to neutralise all evil plans against me;
Just as you will neutralise
Any evil, that I might be tempted;
To plan against my fellow men;
Because as you have proclaimed;

That is the universal secret;
Of long life and enduring prosperity.
Protect me today as always from all dangers;
And evils in my abode, place of work, and in my interactions with others.
(Add any other special desire for the day);
And touch the ground with your head in obeisance to Orunmila. That is what he does to God every morning which earned him the title of Ajiborisa kpero. That is, the divinity who wakes up every morning to give thanks and prayers to the Almighty God, on behalf of himself, all his children and followers. That is why he has enjoined his adherents to do the same to him every morning. As long as they are able to offer such prayers in good faith and conviction, he promised to protect them throughout their lives.

When this Odu appears at divination, for a man who already has his own Ifa, he should be told that he has merely taken his Ifa and abandoned it in obscurity. Ifa is annoyed with him because he will only have the strength to protect the person from his enemies and from the ferocious divinities, if he serves him in good faith. On the other hand, if the Odu comes out for a man, who does not already have his own Ifa, he will be advised to have one without any further delay, because death and misfortune are already on his trail and only Orunmila can save him, from the imminent catastrophe.

The prize of ingratitude:

When Oyeku-Etura got to the world, he was a successful Ifa priest, although he was not wealthy enough to buy a horse. He had six surrogates who were indentured to him to learn the art and practice of Ifism. After gaining proficiency, they were subsequently ordained as Ifa priests. They soon became very successful and wealthy but only by manipulating Ifa's mode of practice to their personal advantages. It is easy to become rich in the practice of Ifa if the priest uses his authority to charge exorbitant fees. Orunmila is never happy with such Ifa priests. That was the setting in which Olofin invited Oyeku-Etura and his six former surrogates to make divination for him on what to do to return prosperity to his kingdom. The six junior awos dressed gorgeously and rode on horses to the palace. But their benefactor and master came in a modest dress and on foot.

At divination, some of the six junior awos recommended sacrifice with cows, plenty of goats, rams, pigs, several bundles of white cloth and 100 bags of money for prosperity to return to the king and country.

While the junior awos were demonstrating their mode of divination, the more knowledgeable and experienced Oyeku-Etura was required to round up the divination. He declared that prosperity had eluded the town because some traditional divinities had not been served for a long time and so they became incapable of stopping misfortune from preventing the children of prosperity from visiting the town. He proclaimed that six awos should be tied up at once for sacrifice to those divinities while he left for the bush to fetch the relevant leaves.

As soon as Oyeku-Etura left for the bush, Olofin gave the command for the six junior awos to be bound in chains awaiting sacrifice. When he returned from the bush, Olofin confirmed to him that the six awos had been tied up for the sacrifice. When he asked for his six colleagues, who were present before he left for the bush, Olofin replied; that they were the ones chained up for the sacrifice. Oyeku-Etura was astonished as he declared that what he prescribed for the sacrifice were 6 guinea fowls which happened to translate to "awo" in Ifa parlance although it also means Ifa priest. He quickly ordered their release and that since it was forbidden to bind an Ifa priest in chains Olofin should give each of them a goat to atone to their Ifa for their shabby treatment. He however, added, the reasons why the six Ifa priests underwent the unfortunate fortuitous treatment was because Orunmila wanted to punish them for prostituting and bastardizing his ethoes and usage. They had been using Ifism for their own selfish benefits in contravention of the altruistic and magnanimous dogmas stipulated by Orunmila. He advised them to refrain from their materialistic and extortionate approach to Ifism, if they were to live long and to avoid the risk of falling from affluence to penury. The six awos were instantly unchained and they thanked Oyeku-Etura, promising to respect Orunmila's dicta and to offer their morning prayers to Orunmila ardently and religiously.

When this Odu comes out at divination for an apparently affluent person, he should be told that he became rich by hook or by crook, and that he has ignored his benefactor and despised his senior colleagues. He should make sacrifice with a goat, 3 aligator pepper and 3 ginger seeds.

He made divination for household utensils.
Oyeku be etula.
Omi nu oko mi kun kun kun.
Aya jimi giri giri.
Adifa fun Orun ligho isilo,
Wongbe Ogan lo si ilu omi,
Woni ki won ru ebo,
Sugbon koru ebo.
Igba nikon loru ebo.

Oyeku be tula made divination for all household utensils when they declared war on the river. They included mortar, piston, plates, bowls, cups, tray, spoon, knife, needle and gourd. They were advised to make sacrifice if they were to come within hailing distance of success in their expedition. All of them, with the exception of the gourd (Igba in Yoruba and Uko in Bini) refused to make the recommended sacrifice.

When they got to the river, they waged a fierce battle on the water. Their onset created whirlpools and vortexes which drowned all the attackers with the exception of the gourd, who stayed afloat on top of the river. When the gourd discovered that all his comrades-in-arms had been swallowed up by the river, he began to rejoice with the song:

Tente maashe yu
Tente maashe boo,

Modupe fun Oyeku betula.

Thus he was rejoicing for surviving the war against the river and giving thanks to his diviner. When it comes out at divination for someone going to war or a mission, fraught with tremendous risk to life, he should be advised to make sacrifice with all available eatable foodstuffs and household utensils which would be packed into a gourd and jettisoned into the river, in order to return safely from the expedition. That is, if it is Uree. If it however comes out as Ayeo, he should be advised to refrain from embarking on the mission.

He made divination for a pregnant woman:
  Agba gba ridi ridi,
  Ko'fi inu han ara 'won,
  Odifa fun oye,
  Nijo tio nloyun

He made divination for a woman called Oye when she was pregnant. When she had a threatened abortion, she went to Orunmila for divination. Unknown to her, another lady called Etura who lived where Oye used to buy kolanuts regularly, had been watching the development of her pregnancy. After knowing that Oye was pregnant even though the pregnancy was neither visible nor obvious to any mortal, Etura worked out a strategy for destroying the pregnancy.

After divination, Orunmila asked Oye who she used to buy kolanuts from regularly. She replied that it was from a friend of hers called Etura. She was subsequently advised to refrain from buying kolanuts, and seeing the woman from then on, because she weas a witch who was gunning for her pregnancy. She was however advised to make sacrifice with a duck because a child does not know when the duck sleeps. That was to neutralise the damage already done by the witch and to arrest the threatened abortion. She made the sacrifice very quickly, and the pregnancy solidified. She subsequently had a successful pregnancy and delivered safely.

When this Odu comes out at divination, the divinee is advised to refrain from buying kolanuts from his or her regular seller or from familiar sources because danger awaits him or her there. If the divinee is a woman, she would be told that she is in her early months of pregnancy and that to avoid any threat to it, she should cease buying kolanuts from a particular seller or place so that the seller might not spoil her pregnancy. She should make sacrifice with a duck.

Divination for purposes of marriage:
  Ma'yileki eru baba mi lonshe,
  Odifa fun Orunmila,
  Nijoti baaba agbon miregun,
  Lo gba omo Olokun,
  She 'rin ade shaya,
  Ebo niki oru.

When Orunmila was proposing to seek the hands of Olokun's daughter in marriage, he requested one of his surrogates called Ma'yileki to make divination for him. He told Orunmila to make sacrifice with a goat, rat, fish, eko and akara. He made the sacrifice.

The girl was subsequently given in marriage to Orunmila. After living together for some time, the bride proposed that it was time for him to visit her father, with her. He readily agreed to the suggestion. As they were travelling by water in a canoe, Orunmila spotted a giant Aro fish. The fish had a big head and carried a red Parrot's feather in its mouth. Thinking that the fish was his father-inlaw, Orunmila bent his knees to greet the fish, but his wife told him not to condescend so low because the fish was only her father's slave. Eventually, Orunmila met Olokun in his divine majesty and prostrated to greet his father-in-law.

He was accorded befitting hospitality. When it was time for them to return home, Olokun ordered his exchequer to bestow the bride and the bride-groom with all items of wealth and prosperity. Thereafter they lived happily in prosperity and affluence.

When this Odu comes out for a man proposing to marry he should be told that the spouse is from the kingdom of Olokun and that he should make the above-mentioned sacrifice because the woman is going to bring prosperity to him. He should therefore proceed to firm up arrangements to marry the girl after making the sacrifice.

Divination for child-birth:

Aiye ti mo rije, lo 'ni,
Oju ti oba lo
Odifa fun Olokoshe atosi,
Lo 'de otu-ife.

That was the name of the Awo who made divination for Olokoshe the pauper of Ife when his wife was pregnant. He was so poor that as his wife approached delivery, he began to wonder how he was going to procure the means of feeding her and the child.

Eventually he took his last money, the equivalent of one kobo and left for Orunmila's place to perform divination for him. When Orunmila heard of his plight, he decided to perform divination for him ex-gratia.

At divination Orunmila advised him to use the money with which he was to pay for divination, to buy a single rat and a single fish for sacrifice. He quickly left for the market to buy the materials and Orunmila made the sacrifice for him free of charge. Orunmila told him that although he was at that time too poor to pay for divination and sacrifice, he would nonetheless be in a position to conveniently return to pay for them after the birth of his in-coming child. That was Orunmila's way of telling him that the unborn child held the key to his prosperity. Finally, Orunmila advised him to go into the forest the following morning in search of whatever he could lay his hands on for sale to raise money.

The following morning, he left for the forest in search of snails to sell. Unknown to him, Esu had commanded all snails and tortoises in heaven and earth to bury themselves beneath the ground. After combing the forest for a long time, he became hungry and tired. He decided to sit by the foot of an oak tree to rest. Shortly afterwards he fell asleep. As he was sleeping, a drip of honey dropped from the top of the tree right into his mouth and he licked it up and he woke up from his sleep. When he opened his eyes, he saw a medley of snails heeped to his front and a file of tortoises to his back. He went on his kneels and thanked God for answering his prayers and for allowing his sacrifice to manifest so quickly. Overwhelmed with gratification, he began to sing in praise of the Awo who made divination and sacrifice for him.

He sang that God heard his prayers and knowing that he was hungry released drops of honey into his mouth and delivered an assemblage of snails and tortoises to give manifestation to his dream. As he moved to collect the snails and the tortoises, he was still singing in praise of his Awo by mentioning his name:

Aiye timorije, timorimu,
Lo ni oju toba lo.

At that point his friend was running from home in search of him to report the wife's safe delivery of twin babies. He told his friend to return home because he was going to collect the snails and the tortoises he found in the forest. Incidentally the friend had clearly over-heard his song of praise which climaxed with the stanza that the favour done to him by God on that day, was more than the Oba or King could ever receive.

His friend left him and made straight for the King's palace to report that Olokoshe the poor man of Ife had blasphemed by saying that the favour he received from God was more than what God could ever give the King. The king angrily gave orders for him to be arrested and arraigned before the royal court.

Meanwhile, he returned home with his snails and tortoises to the jubilation of his new born twins. As he was rejoicing for the multiple blessings he had received in one day, the royal police arrived at his house to arrest him for the offence of using profane language. When he was asked to explain his blasphemous proclamation, he narrated how he left home that morning in search of snails to sell for money to feed his pregnant wife and how he got snails and tortoises with honey dropping into his mouth. After listening to him attentively, the king agreed with him that God had actually bestowed on him more favour than he the king could ever expect, because he could neither go to the forest in search of snails nor have the opportunity of sleeping in the forest for honey to drop into his mouth. The king then delivered a verdict of non-prosecuti and he was acquitted and discharged and told to return home to rejoice over his blessings from God.

That incident gave him the opportunity of realising the type of friend he had. When he returned home however, he immediately took the snails and the tortoises to the market for sale.

That moment coincided with the time when the daughter of Olokun was having a difficult labour in heaven. Olokun's diviners had hurriedly been invited in heaven to find out why his daughter was having a difficult labour and they had recommended sacrifice with a tortoise and a snail. Olokun's messengers had combed the forest of heaven and earth in search of the snails and tortoises without success, because unknown to anyone, Esu had conjured all the snails and tortoises in heaven and earth to conceal themselves beneath the ground.

After combing the length and breadth of heaven for the sacrificial materials, they moved to the boundary of heaven and earth, and used their esoteric binoculars to target the availability of snails and tortoises any where on earth. They could not locate any. Fortunately however, they targetted Olokoshe carrying some snails and tortoises in a basket to the market.

The heavenly messengers quickly telescoped the distance and made a quick rendezvous with Olokoshe just before he got to the market. When they met him, they asked him the price at which he was prepared to sell his wares. At that juncture, Esu transfigured into a chief and assumed overlordship over Olokoshe who he ordered to keep quiet. The chief told the messengers from heaven that the carrier of the snails and tortoises was his servant and that only he the Chief could negotiate the price of the materials. He then enumerated the price of each snail as 16 men, 16 women, cows, 16 goats, 16 fowls and 16 bags of money. On the other hand he gave the price of each tortoise as a hundred sacks of beads, a hundred pieces of white cloth, and a hundred bags of money. The divine messengers asked the Chief and his servant to wait for them and that they would return with the prizes presently.

In a matter of minutes, they returned with the asking prizes, collected 2 snails and 2 tortoises, and returned to heaven. Olokoshe was totally confounded. It was after the prizes had been paid, that the chief revealed his identity and told him to take all of them home as the reward for his sacrifice. When he told Esu to take any part he liked from the prizes, he only took one he-goat and disappeared from sight. Before he got home however, Olokoshe sent two of each of the items to Orunmila to atone for the divination and sacrifice he did for him ex-gratia. True to the prediction at divination, the newly born twins had brought prosperity to their parents from heaven, and Olokoshe was later made the second-in-command to the king - the Shashere of Ife. At the same time Orunmila got multiple recompense for his earlier magnanimity to Olokoshe.

When it comes out at divination for a pregnant woman or for a man having an expectant wife, the person should be told that the end of his or her days of penury is in sight provided he made the requisite sacrifice. The expectant woman is likely to deliver twins who are navigating their parents' prosperity from heaven. He should make sacrifice with snails and tortoise after which he would have a dream which would show him what to do in order to have his wishes to manifest. If the man does not already have his own Ifa, he should arrange to have one without any delay, at least to perform the initial ceremony of putting the Ifa seeds into a put of palm oil. That initial ceremony should be performed if possible before the wife puts to birth.

DIVINATION FOR THE WOODEN SPOON AND THE SLEDGE HAMMER:

Akpa agbe oun lon kpinrin,
Alugbe oun luke le lu obe,

Adifa fun Oowu abufun Igi Sibi.

These were the awos who made divination for Ogun's sledge hammer (Oowu in yoruba and Umomo in Bini), as well as for the wooden spoon for stiring soup (Igi sibi in yoruba or Uruenhen in Bini) when they were coming from heaven. Ogun's sledge hammer was advised to make sacrifice with roasted yam, yellow melon (elegede in yoruba and eyen in Bini) and palm oil to serve her guardian angel in order to avoid having a pregnancy she will never be able to deliver. She failed to make the sacrifice.

On her part, the wooden spoon was advised to make sacrifice with palm oil, the chaff of palm fruits used for igniting fire and the flames of fire in order to win the battle she was bound to have with heat on earth. when the sledge hammer got to the world she got married to Ogun who asked her to assist him in manufacturing his wares. Her figure was at the time very slim and straight. Not long after, she became pregnant, but could not deliver the foetus. That is why she has remained pregnant to this day because she failed to make the prescribed sacrifice. On the other hand, the wooden spoon got married to the cooking pot and the world found her very useful for stiring soup on the fire. Inspite of the heat that the cooking pot generated, she survived it without being burnt, due to the sacrifice she made in heaven.

When this Odu comes out at divination for a man, he should be told to make sacrifice so that his wife might not have a difficult pregnancy which could be generated by heat in the womb. Ditto for a woman.

HE MADE DIVINATION FOR ARIGBONRON:

Oyeku-ba-Etura made divination for Arigbonron, who became crippled when he was going to inherit his father's legacy. He was told to make sacrifice with; a he-goat to Esu, cock to Ogun, and cock to Sango, in order to enjoy his inheritance in good health and long life. His parents were already dead and he was their only surviving son. He did not make the sacrifices. However, he inherited his father's house and the parents' heirlooms.

Not long afterwards, Esu stood one morning at the boundary of heaven and earth and asked:
Agbo lere afakan;
and his friend Ighoroko answered
Oke lere ewe,
Ogbo lere ajigede,
Arigbonron ni won ni
Ki o ru ebo,
Sugbon koru ebo na.

This Odu provides the opportunity of demonstrating the danger of failing or refusing, to make any sacrifice prescribed at divination. Through his friend Ighoroko, Esu is able to target all those who have refused to make sacrifices after divination. Ighoroko, the bosom friend of Esu is his path-finder and seer. It is Ighoroko alone who has the means of identifying all the citizens of heaven and earth who had been told at divination to make sacrifice.

As soon as the cock crows every morning, Esu-Obadara takes position at Orita-Ijaloko, that is, the boundary of heaven and earth to ask his friend who had been told to make sacrifice but refused to do it. Ighoroko will immediately identify the names and locations of all those who have refused to make sacrifices in heaven and on earth. Esu will react by creating problems for them until reason or force of circumstances compels them to make the recommended sacrifices.

It was against the foregoing backdrop that Esu was told that Arigbonron had bluntly refused to make the sacrifice prescribed for him. Esu reacted by going to persuade Ogun and Sango to incapacitate one of his legs and one of his hands. Before then, he was an able-bodied person, stoutly built, and without any physical deformity.

Thereafter, Ogun began to watch Arigbonron. As soon as Ogun caught up with him, he broke one of his legs. Soon afterwards, Sango also met him and deformed one of his hands. Ogun broke his right leg while Sango deformed his left hand. Thereafter, the now-deformed Arigbonron began to sing:

Ule baba mi ree Arigbonron,
Ron ron ron Arigbonron.
That is the noise that any person deformed on one legs
makes to this day as he or she treads on the ground.

When this Odu comes out at divination for a person whois about to inherit any legacy, he should be advised to serve Esu, Ogun and Sango to avoid the danger of physical deformity.

THE PRIZE OF CONCEIT AND CONTEMPT:

Ifa Oyeku-ba-tu-la,
kofe kofe Awo Ode egba,
Kofe kofe Awo ode Ijesha
Ofo koto, ofo ko rowo
Ofo gbagede afo mo,
Oju moki babalawo, iku iwere
Baba ilaji ni o nshe,
Eru Oni Ife
Abure baba ilaji siko
Woni dida owo,
Osi kowon ni tite ile,
Osi kowon ni ebo sise.

These were the names of the six Ifa priests, educated by Baba Ilaji, who made divination for the King of Ife. Baba Ilaji became an Ifa priest after he was released from slavery. After becoming an adept in Ifa art and practice, he also taught many students in IFISM. One day, he was invited by the Olofin of Ife to make divination for him. He also met six Ifa priests who he had taught much earlier. When he greeted them, with the call sign of ABORU ABOYE, they failed to answer with the traditional reply of ABOYE ABOSISE. Although he was their teacher, nonetheless they looked down on him because he was once their father's slave. Without showing his anger he proceeded to do divination for Olofin. After divination he told Olofin that the reason for his problems was that they had not made sacrifice for a long time. He declared that sacrifice had to be made almost immediately, with 6 awos. Meanwhile, after making the declaration, Baba Ilaji sneaked out of the room, as if he wanted to go and ease himself. He did not return.

Olofin immediately gave instruction for the six young Awos in the room to be bound in chains awaiting sacrifice. After waiting in vain for Baba Ilaji to return, Olofin sent messengers to fetch him. When he returned to find the six Awos in chains, he queried Olofin for daring to bind Ifa priests in chains and asked whether he did not realise that anyone or any place that binds an Awo in chains will know no peace and tranquility until they are released and compensated. He demanded to know what offence the six awos had committed.

Olofin however explained that he (Baba Ilaji) was the one who prescribed that the sacrifice had to be made with six awos and since the six young awos had made themselves available he thought it was a welcomed coincidence. Baba Ilaji explained that he meant that sacrifice had to be made with six guinea fowls. He therefore ordered the release of the Ifa priests and a strong apology was made by the Olofin to them. They were however happy that their lives were spared, thanks to their teacher and mentor.

When this odu appears at divination, the person should be advised not to show disrespect to a higher authority. He should be told not to deride an elderly person no matter how lowly placed. He should however make sacrifice with a guinea fowl.

OYEKU-BE-ETULA CAME TO THE WORLD AS THE SON OF JAGUN:

His father was an itinerant and ubiquitous masquerade (egun dancer). While at home on one occasion, the father co-habited with his mother after her menstruation. Thereafter he went away dancing in several towns and villages. He was absent when the wife became pregnant and when the child was born. He was neither home when the child grew up nor when he became an adult. The father was also fond of drinking and had the weakness of swapping his belongings for drinks.

His son grew up to become a masquerade dancer like his father. He too took to itinerant dancing. Once upon a time, he came to a town where his father had just left after his masquerade rounds. He over-heard a comment in the town that he was a better dancer than the masquerade who visited the town the previous day. He continued his journey until he met his father at another town without recognising him. As the young masquerade was dancing, his father over-heard complimentary remarks about the superior dancing capabilities of the younger dancer. The comments invoked the envy and jealousy of the more elderly masquerade, who swore to eliminate the young dancer at the earliest opportunity, not knowing it was his own son.

Eventually, the two masquerades met and began to dance. The younger masquerade danced so impressively that the elder masquerade could not continue his dancing. As he sat down to watch the young masquerade, he began to conjure the rain with the following incantation:

Erin folami,
Oruko tan npe Olorun oji,
Amenu fefe ogu ere,
Akola ma labee oruko yekpe fufu.

As soon as he finished the incantation the clouds gathered and the rain began to threaten. The younger masquerade sensing what had happened, countermanded by saying:

Ikan won ma diyi mi ka,
Oji fefe wonbo lono,
Mokpe e egbe egbe oje,
Mokpo rada ora da kon ofisi,
Iya a'isi baba mi nle,
Omo ajimuda dogo nile,
Olotin, egbe gbemi.

The father then saw the Son suspended in the air and refrained as follows:

Ajaguna gbidede,
Tewe tima koro.

and the young masquerade came down. The elder masquerade then invited the younger one to a corner for a te-te-a-te-te. There was no rain but there was severe gale force wind and people had started running helter-skelter.

The two masquerades went aside and removed their head masks. Jagun asked the younger man where he came from and he replied that he came from Igbo-Ona the land of Jagun where he pregnated his mother, who had not seen him since he was born. Asked for the name of his father, he replied that it was Jagun whereunto he identified himself as Jagun.

Thereafter, they moved to a private corner to remove their masks. The son asked him whether he was Jagun Agbagbu Olomosho. The father began to cry. He said that he did not know that his wife Emerogho had brought forth a son old enough to challenge him. He said there and then that his dancing days were over, and decided to return home immediately.

When this Odu appears at Ugbodu the person is likely to be a musician, and his father is not likely to have been available to bring him up. Unless sacrifice is made his father will not live for more than three years after the Ifa initiation ceremony. He should serve the Ifa with a ram. He should make a feast or sacrifice to the secret cult to which he belongs.

At ordinary divination, the person should make sacrifice to the night and give he-goat to Esu to avoid losing a child, not to death but not to be missing.

Chapter 12
OYEKU - BI - IRETE
OYEKE - BI - IRETE - SILE - AJE

I	II
I	II
II	II
I	II

Oyeku-Bi-Irete is traditionally a provider of wealth and prosperity. When it comes out at Ugbodu during initiation, the person is sure to prosper in life if the appropriate sacrifices are made on time.

HE MADE DIVINATION FOR THE DAUGHTER OF OLOKUN WHEN SHE WAS COMING FROM HEAVEN.

When the daughter of Olokun was leaving for earth, she went to Teetee for divination on what to do to prosper on earth. He advised her to offer sacrifice with a Pigeon to her head, and to offer a guinea-fowl to her guardian angel (Eleda or Ehi). She was to make the sacrifice not only to enable her wealth to accompany her to the world, but also to enable her meet her rightful husband on earth. If she married the rightful husband on earth, she would give birth to a son who would be more prosperous, more popular, and more famous than the parents. She made the sacrifice.

Back on earth, Orunmila was also advised at divination to offer a he-goat to Esu, a pigeon to his head, and a guinea-fowl to his Ifa in order to come across his rightful wife who would bring greatness and prosperity to him. Meanwhile, Olokun's daughter set out on her journey to earth where she landed at Oja-Ajigbomekun Akira i.e. the market at boundary between heaven and earth.

Orunmila had offered a he-goat to Esu but set out for the market to buy a pigeon and a guinea fowl for the other sacrifice. When he got to the market, he bought the 2 birds and was about to return home with them when he saw a pretty woman, dressed in immaculate white. He stopped to admire the woman who also focused her gaze on him. Their eyes met and they both smiled at each other. The woman asked him what he was going to do with the birds he had in hand. Orunmila explained that he was going to use them for sacrifice to his head and his Ifa. The woman told him that it was a happy coincidence that she too had used the same birds for making sacrifice before leaving home. The woman was already head-over-heels in love with Orunmila who also requited the woman's affection. Meanwhile, the girl offered to go and know his house. By the time they got to Orunmila's house it was getting dark and he lost no time in making the sacrifices. Thereafter, the woman cooked the food for the sacrifice and they invited friends to enjoy it with them. They spent the night together. Two weeks later, the woman decided to return home but Orunmila persuaded her to stay a little longer. She however insisted that she was not a loner, that she had many followers who traditionally accompanied her to the market. She promised to return as soon as she completed her domestic chores at home. Orunmila escorted her half-way and returned.

Not long afterward, Orunmila had a dream in which he saw the children of prosperity (Ala or Uwa) trooping into his house. When he woke up in the morning, he sounded Ifa who disclosed to him to paint the inner Chamber of his house with white chalk in order to provide a befitting abode to the visitor he was to have. He did so accordingly. Twenty-one days later, the woman returned in the company of several men and women carrying luggages on their heads. The woman was happy to see the house properly renovated to her taste. It was at that point that the Lady disclosed her identity as the daughter of Olokun - the divinity of water, and that she had come to marry him for keeps, because her diviner had told her that he was her rightful husband. He too readily agreed to marry her because, Ifa had revealed to him that she was his rightful wife. Later that evening, Olokun's daughter disclosed to Orunmila that she missed her menstruation at the end of her monthly cycle.

Every five days thereafter, the followers of the woman often left for the market to return with all descriptions of treasures, inlcuding beads, clothes, Brass, and lead, which made the family to become exceedingly rich.

Nine months later, she gave birth to a male child who was called Money (Owo or Igho). Money became everybody's favourite child and companion and true to divination prediction, he became more famous than his parents throughout the earth.

When this Odu comes out at Ugbodu, the person will be told that he is yet to marry a wife who will bring prosperity to his life, and that the wife will give birth to a child who will be universally famous and popular. He should be advised to prepare an image of Olokun to be placed on his Ifa shrine. At divination the man should be advised to have his own Ifa and for woman to marry a man with his own Ifa.

HE ALSO MADE DIVINATION FOR SANGO:

Sango had 3 children called Ojo-Akitikori, Ige-Adumbi, and Dada-Awuru. He also had several relations who were big and tall. When Sango became ill, he went to Oyeku-bi-Irete for divination. He was told to make sacrifice to avoid becoming seriously ill enough to be taken away to a healing home. He did not make the sacrifice. He was eventually taken away from home. He had problems with his leg and the doctor who cured him asked for the equivalent of 5k as the cost of treatment. Sango did not have the money. He decided to send messages to his brothers who happened to be the tall trees in the forest of heaven viz: IROKO, OAK, OBECHE, AGBA, etc. None of them agreed to contribute to his assistance. Out of frustration, he sent another message to his children and the eldest of them Dada, (Alaro in yoruba or Okhere in Bini) contributed the money with the assistance of his junior brothers OJO and IGE, and they sent the money to their father.

As Sango was returning home now hail and hearty, there was a tornado followed by lightning and thunder-storm which provided the prelude for him to identify and destroy all his brothers who failed to respond to his distress call for help. He up-rooted all the big trees and set them on fire. Since he was already charged for combat, when he reached the home of the young palm tree (Dada or Agbihiagba), Sango folded his hands and branches and Dada asked:

> To ba ron ti.
> Ojo ke te.
> Ko ron ti
> Ojo ke te,
> Ko ron ti
> Ojo ti ko ko
> Merin di logun she mu
> Nile Alaroye, Omo araye lomu-oo.

With that cry, Sango recognised his son and left him alone untouched. In the same vein, he also left IGE (Igbaghon) and OJO (Igiawegboto) untouched. That is why Thunder never destroys these plants in the forest to this day.

At Ugbodu, the person will be told to take good care of his first three children because they will come to his rescue at a critical moment in his life. If he does not already have a child who is Dada or Agbihiagha - i.e a person with coiled-hair, he can look for one in his family and stay close to him or her. He must not rely for any support on his great and wealthy brothers because they will abandon him in his hour of need. If he does not already have a thunder-stone in his Ifa shrine, he should provide one without delay because, Sango will help him to fight his enemies in future. He should also provide one cutlass for his Ifa shrine.

At ordinary divination, the person should be told to offer he-goat to Esu to prevent illness, and that he must avoid coming into close contact with a lunatic, because he might injure him.

WHY THIS ODU IS CALLED OYEKU-BI-IRETE-SILE-AJE:

When this Odu comes out at divination, the person should be told that his eldest brother is planning to do him in. Nonetheless, he should be advised not to keep him at arms length because whatever evil the brother plots against him might hatch into a blessing in disguise. That is why it is often said that there is a soul of goodness in things evil.

This Odu made divination for Oyeku and Irete. They were both two brothers living on earth. Oyeku was the senior of the two. On one occasion, Oyeku decided to send Irete alone to the market of Oja-Ajigbomekan. Irete however decided to make a divination on account of a dream he had the previous night in which he found himself falling into a ravine. He decided to make divination and Oyeku-bi-Irete came out. He was required to make sacrifice with a he-goat to Esu and to serve his head with a Pigeon. He made the sacrifice.

As he set out for the market the following day, Oyeku advised him not to take the usual route to the market, but to take a short circuit, where unknown to Irete, but well known to Oyeku, a crater had been dug and covered with leaves. No one could pass that route without falling into the bottomless crater. Unsuspectingly, Irete followed the advice of his elder brother and took the danger-laden-short-cut.

Meanwhile however, after eating his he-goat, Esu proceeded to line the bottom of the crater with bags of money covered with a layer of feathers. As Irete was walking along the route, he fell into the precipice. As his heart was about to fail him, he discovered that he landed on a soft layer of feathers. When he tried to struggle out of the hole, his feet treaded on some hard substance and upon closer examination, he discovered that it was money. He finally succeeded in coming out of the crater and began to remove the money to his house. After getting all the money to his house, he however gave part of it to OYEKU whose evil contrivance brought him to his new found wealth.

He then made a thanksgiving feast to which all and sundry were invited. At the height of the merriment, he began to sing:-

Ibi re re le ni, Eni bi ni si,
Gbemi leke, gbemi leke, ibi rere.
Lo kpe, gbemi ire, Ibi rere.

He was rejoicing because the death planned for him had landed him in everlasting prosperity.

When this Odu comes out at divination, the person will be told that an elderly friend or relation of his will give him an evil-intentioned advice. Before acting on it however, he must make sacrifice to Esu and his head, because he will prosper by following the advice.

HE MADE DIVINATION FOR THE HUMAN GENITALS TO PRODUCE CHILDREN:

Okpokun Orokun
Adifa fun Oko
Abufun Obo,
Nijo ti awon mejeji
Fi omi oju shu,
Bere Omo tuurutu.

He made divinatioin for the Penis and the Vulva when they were both crying for a child. They were both advised to make sacrifice. The Vulva (Obo or Uhe) was told to make sacrifice with a hen, rabbit and guinea-fowl. On the other hand, the Penis (Oko or Fkia) was told to make sacrifice with a cock, dog, and 4 snails. They both made the sacrifices.

When they got home, the Vulva opened her mouth and the penis entered and they both began to sing in praise of the Awo who made divination and sacrifice for them. Their song chanted as follows:-

Okpoku Oroku

Okpoku Oroku:

That is the noise made by the sexual organs to this day during cohabitation. Thereafter, they began to have children. At divination for someone in dare need of a child the man should make the sacrifice made by the penis and the woman should make the sacrifice the Vulva made.

DIVINATION FOR LONG LIFE:

When Orunmila got to the world, the people he met asked him to divine on what to do in order to enjoy the good things of life in peace, long life and prosperity.

The following dialogue ensued:-

Orunmila ni goro; Moni oye o n'bi,
Oni igbati oye nbi, O to ki ire aje wo Ile wa.
Orunmila ni goro; moni oye n'bi,
Oni igbati oye n'bi, o to ki ire aya, Wo ile wa.
Orunmila ni goro; Moni oye n'bi,
Oni igbati oye n'bi, o to ki ire omo wo ile wa.
Orunmila ni goro, Moni Oye n'bi
Oni igbati oye n'bi, o toki gbogbo ire, wo ile wa.

Orunmila advised them to use Pigeon and white pudding (Ekuru-funfun in yoruba or Emieki-no-fua in Bini) to make sacrifice for prosperity, a big cock for wisdom, a rabbit for child birth, and a sheep (Agunton in yoruba or Iyo-Ohuan in Bini) for long life. Agunton is used with the appropriate leaves to bury the danger of untimely death. This is a major sacrifice (Ono-Ifa in yoruba or Ode-Iha in Bini), which must be made as soon as this Odu appears for any one during initiation into Ifism at Ugbodu.

If this sacrifice is made and the image of Olokun is prepared for the Ifa shrine, as well as inserting a thunder-stone in the Ifa plate, the person will triumph in the many battles he will fight in life. He will be very prosperous, have many children, and live to a ripe old age. He should however refrain from eating the meat of Rabbit, and any food prepared with bitter-leaf.

HE MADE DIVINATION FOR OLOFIN:

There reigned an Olofin in Ife who was very dictatorial and did not know how to blend fear and love as instruments of governance. He only relied on the use of fear for ruling his people. A good ruler should know when to inter-lace fear and love in political management. He distanced himself so much from his people that he became surrounded by sychophants and praise singers who only told him what he was pleased to hear rather than the truth. Those who were capable of telling him the bitter truth had all been marginalised into keeping him at arms-length. He therefore had no one to foreward him when his people were planning a popular insurrection. Before he knew what was going on, his entire kingdom had revolted against him and the people were calling for his banishment from the throne. It was at that stage that he invited Oyeku-Bi-Irete for divination.

Oyeku lo bi-Irete si le Aje

Ofi erun eshi kowon le run,
Ada fa fun Olofin,
Ooma she ofun ton.

He advised Olofin after divination to make sacrifice with a ram and a goat, and to give a he-goat to Esu. The sacrifice was made on the eve of a violent demonstration which the people had planned to make the following day. On the night of the sacrifice, Esu came out with his followers, and they began to sing war songs, warning everybody that any one who dared to demonstrate against the king would not only lose his life, but also his first born child. In the refrain to the war Song, Esu advised the citizenry to send a delegation to the King to vent their grievances. At the same time, Esu went to Olofin to advise him to make a feast with a cow, a ram, and a goat for his entire people and to request them to take the opportunity for the feast to mirror his own wrong-doings to him.

No one dared to come out of his house the following day and the proposed demonstration became a-non-starter. At noon on that day, the king sent out his royal heralds to make a royal proclamation that the king was ready for a re-approachment with the people of the kingdom to be preceeded that evening with a feast to which all and sundry were invited. Following the feast and settlement, there was general reconciliation throughout the kingdom between king and subjects. Eventually, peace and prosperity returned to the kingdom, and the Olofin reigned in concord and harmony to a ripe old age.

When this Odu comes out at divination for a person in authority, he should be advised that his subordinates are dis-satisfied with his style of management. He should make a feast with a ram and a goat and give a he-goat to Esu, in order to avert the risk of rebellion against him.

HE MADE DIVINATION FOR THE HEAD

Agbagba ni da agbado sile. Abo ni won fi bo ra won loju. Adifa fun Ori t'i onfi omi oju shu bere ure gbogbo. Ebo ki afi akiko adiye ati eyele bo ori.

The elders threw corn on the ground as if they were making magic with them. They are the names of the Awos who made divination for the Head when he was poor and crying for prosperity. He was advised to make sacrifice with cock and pigeon. He did the sacrifice and all the other parts of the body came to seek protection and leadership from him.

At divination, the person should be told that he is a group leader. Although he may be poor now, if he makes sacrifice with a he-goat to Esu and serves his head with a pigeon, his destiny will manifest.

Chapter 13
OYEKU-BE-EKA

```
  II   II
  I    II
  II   II
  II   II
```

OYEKU and EKA were two brothers (Twins) who left heaven for the world at the same time. Before leaving heaven, they were told to make sacrifice to avoid the problem of untimely death. The names of the Awos who made divination for them were:

Ayejin, Ayejin Aye gbe Agere,
Ude ni non'Okpa Tere ko,
Oji gada godo ninu, Agogo Odee.

They were advised to feast the divinities with a goat and to give he-goat to Esu before leaving heaven. They did the sacrifices. Oyeku was the first to arrive and so, became the senior of the two. They were advised in heaven to mind their business on earth. They grew up in the practice of Ifa art. They built their house on the bank of the river where they lived. THE TWO BROTHERS ARRANGED TO TRAVEL OUT FOR IFA PRACTICE TO ESI-ILAWO:

The name of the Awo who made divination for them before leaving for ESI-ILAWO was:-

Ifa-Oyeku-Be-Eka je Eyi kekere Iya.
Ki 'o ma ba je Eyi nla
Tete je wo mu womu.

They were advised neither to be greedy nor to be extortionate if they were to maximise the gains from their mission.

When they got to the town, they were lodged in separate accommodations. Before leaving home, they were advised to serve Esu with a he-goat, and to make sacrifice with 2 pigeons, lamp, soap, beach-sand and River sand, and the leaves of Egbawo (Oghohen leaves in Bini). Oyeku refused to make the sacrifice, but Eka did it on his own.

They were receiving clients in their separate lodgings. On his part, Oyeku was demanding very high fees for his consultations. His consultation fee was never less than one bag of money or 50k. His exorbitant charges soon reduced his flow of clients to a trickle.

On his part, Eka was satisfied with anything between the equivalent of one and five kobo, as a result of which his place was streaming torrentially with an insurge of clients. The flow of clients became so much that he scarcely had time to eat, rest, or sleep.

After seventeen days, they decided to return home. The compensation and gifts received by Eka were so much that they filled a whole boat. On his part, all the collections of OYEKU did not fill a small purse. He became very jealous of his junior brother.

Meanwhile, they set out on their home-ward journey in a canoe. When they got to the depth of the river, Oyeku became over-awed with morbid intentions. He asked Eka to fetch water for him to drink from the river. As EKA bent over the canoe to fetch the water, OYEKU pushed him and he fell and immediately drowned into the bottom of the River. That is how this Odu got its name of OYEKU-BE-EKA-LO-OMI or Oyeku pushed Eka into the River.

Satisfied that Eka was drowned and dead, Oyeku paddled the canoe home alone. When he got home, everybody applauded him for the elaborate canoe-load of gifts he brought, which he described as the product of his proficiency. When they however asked for the whereabouts of Eka, Oyeku replied falsely that they went in different directions because, he lacked the competence to divine like himself in the first town they went together. That was why, he continued, Eka decided to go elsewhere for Ifa practice in his own way.

Their father however, did not believe OYEKU's story partly because he knew that EKA was a better Ifa Priest than OYEKU and mainly due to the fact that he (their father) taught Eka by himself. Oyeku however, off-loaded the contents of Eka's canoe into his house, after distributing some of them as gifts to members of the family.

Back in the River, Eka struggled to resurface on the water and began to repeat the following incantation while still having his Ifa seeds (IKIN or IKEN) tied round his waist.

>Akpa wo mi Amidi galata
>Oke domi amuru golo to
>Maa jeri wo shengbe
>Egba so wo galata gbami - o.

A monkey on top of a tree heard Eka's words and quickly jumped onto an (Agbawa or Oghohen tree) bending over the river. The monkey and a branch of the tree jettisoned into the river. The impact of the tree-branch and the monkey coincided with the third time the river had thrown Eka to the surface and he quickly held on to the tail of the monkey. With the support of the tree-branch, the monkey swam to the safety of the river bank. Eka, now completely exhausted, fell to the ground and fainted.

As if to work for the he-goat given to him much earlier by Eka, Esu conjured a gale-force-wind followed by a drizzle of rain which eventually revived Eka to regain consciousness. Not knowing where he was, he felt his waist and the Ikin or Iken was still there. He consulted it and his own Odu came out. Ifa told him that he would know his way home provided he was not in a hurry. Ifa advised him to stay where he was because help would come instantly. Soon afterwards, a herd of pigs came to the river to drink water. After drinking water, he pursued them by following their path which took him to the back of his father's house. He entered the house and asked for food. After eating, he narrated his experience with Oyeku to his father. At that time, Oyeku was away to the farm. Later in the evening their father sent for Oyeku while telling Eka to hide in the room.

When Oyeku finally returned to the house, their father asked him how they were going to arrange to bring Eka back home. Oyeku replied that Eka was too daft to understand, let alone practise the art of divination and that nobody should worry about him. In an apparent mood of melancholy, their father buried his head between his hands and cried out the name of his beloved son EKA who then came out to the astonishment of OYEKU. It was Oyeku's turn to bury his head in shame.

The matter soon came to the notice of Olofin who ordered the immediate arrest of Oyeku for trial before the council of elders. He was instantly found guilty and condemned to be executed. EKA however, went on his knees to beg for his brother's life to be spared. His entreaty was respected and Oyeku's life was spared, but he subsequently felt too ashamed to continue to face the world. He then repeated an incantation which turned him into a Boa and he crawled into the forest where he lived ever-after. On the other hand, Eka became very rich and prosperous.

As soon as this Odu appears at Ugbodu, the person should be told to immediately wash his head with a he-goat on Esu shrine. He should offer another goat to his Ifa, and serve his head with the meat of monkey and Pig while backing his Ifa shrine. He should collect 61 leaves of Egbawo or Ogbohen which should be mashed with the blood of the he-goat to wash his head on the shrine of Esu in order to ward off or minimise the danger to his life which is bound to be contrived against him by his elder relation.

He should be advised never to travel anywhere in the company of anyone to obviate the risk of death during the trip. If he must go, he should make sacrifice before leaving home.

At ordinary divination, the person should be advised to offer he-goat to Esu to avoid unnecessary contest with some one else on what rightly belongs to him.

EKA PAYS THE PRICE OF FAME AND PROSPERITY:

The work which Eka did in the town of Esi-Ilawo made him famous all over the kingdom of Ife. At that time, there was general famine and deprivation throughout the kingdom. Olofin invited all the prominent Awos in the kingdom to divine on how to end the socio-economic problem afflicting the kingdom. Eka was deliberately excluded by the more elderly Awos from answering the invitation of the King. At the mass divination which the elderly Awos did for the Olofin, they revealed rather spuriously and unscrupulously that the problem of the kingdom would only be solved by offering as sacrifice to the water divinity an impostor-Awo called Eka. The king immediately ordered Eka to be arrested. He was arrested and Eka was brought in ropes to the palace. The other Awos prepared the sacrifice and with hands and feet bound in ropes, Eka was thrown with the sacrifice into the water. While the sacrifice was being made, a herd of bush pigs was watching closely waiting to cross the river. As soon as they entered the River, they saw Eka floating helplessly on the surface of the water. They immediately recognized him as the man who pursued them some years before without harming any of their flock. They realized that he had neither hunted for them nor set any trap to catch any of them. They recognised him as a man who always had a soft heart for animals. The swines joined forces pulled him out of the water and used their teeth to remove the ropes binding him.

In the light of the difficulties which he had encountered in the hands of his fellow Awos, he decided to build a hut near the river, and live the rest of his life in recluse or total seclusion from mankind. Since it is however forbidden to bind an Awo in chains, the socio-economic problems of Ife, instead of abating, was aggravated. For a whole year, there were no new pregnancies in the kingdom. And women already pregnant failed to deliver, while others suffered miscarriages. There had been no rain in the kingdom, for years as a result of which all the harvests failed, which gave rise to draught and famine.

One day, as he went out into the forest in search of food, he saw some women who came to fetch water from the river because all the wells of Ife had dried up. For not having appeared to anyone for a long time, he was already looking like a lunatic. He told the women to warn the Olofin that an Ifa priest would advise him to make sacrifice with a bush pig. He told them to warn the Olofin not to make the sacrifice because if he did, the result would be disastrous. If he killed the bush pig, his house would go up in flames and his eldest daughter would die, all within a span of five days.

After getting the message, the women made straight for the palace where they immediately delivered the message from "a mad-man in the forest." The king retorted that he had no time to listen to the forebodings of a madman.

The following morning, a visiting Ifa Priest made divination for the Olofin and advised him to offer sacrifice with a bush pig to Ifa in order to solve the problems of the kingdom. Since the Priest's prescription coincided with the message from "the mad-man in the forest", Olofin refused to make the sacrifice. The following day, a pig ran from the forest into the palace of Olofin and it was pursued vigorously by the pages of the palace. As they tried to kill it, the feet of the pig touched off a burning fire-wood which immediately fell on the pack of clothes heaped for washing, igniting a ball of flames and setting the harem of the palace ablaze.

The eldest daughter of the king ran into the inner chamber of the palace in fright to tell her father what was hapenning. In the process, she knocked her foot against the door and fell down, dead.

That was the point at which the king remembered the message of the "mad-man in the forest." He sent for him at once. When the messengers got to Eka's hut, they delivered the king's message and told him how his predictions had already manifested. He ran quickly to the palace, where he repeated an incantation that put out the burning fire. With the leaves he plucked from the forest, he squizzed them between his palms, and with another incantation, he dropped the water from it into the eyes of the dead princess, with words which approximated to:

When one falls asleep,
One wakes up after sleeping

And called the Princess's name seven times and stretched his divination staff (Uranke) at her, and she opened her eyes, after regaining consciousness. Thereafter he recommended that Olofin's Ifa should be served with a ram and 200 snails by the side of the River after giving a he-goat to Esu. He predicted that if a heavy rain did not fall before the king returned from the river, he (Eka) should be instantly executed. He added that the rain would mark the beginning of the return of peace and prosperity to the entire kingdom.

Arrangements were made for the sacrifice to be made without any delay. As soon as the king's Ifa was served at the bank of the river, the rain began to threaten. By the time they left for home, a heavy rain-storm had begun, and both king and all members of the sacrificial party were heavily drenched before they got home.

Soon afterwards, all the dormant pregnancies began to re-develop. The folliage of farm crops began to blossom. With a space of one month, over 200 women delivered safely in the town of Ife alone and 25 of the king's wives delivered safely. Prosperity had returned to the town and Eka was made the Chief Diviner of the kingdom.

When this Odu appears at Ugbodu or divination, the person will be told to persevere because the path to his prosperity will be very bumpy and rugged. If he makes the appropriate sacrifice, he will triumph over his enemies. He should refrain from eating the meat of monkey and pig, and should never take to any form of hunting or trap setting for games.

OYEKU-LE-ETURUKPON

```
II  II
II  II
I   II
II  II
```

HOW ORUNMILA BECAME THE CUSTODIAN OF ALL EXISTENCE:

It was Oyeku-Ba-Eturukpon who revealed how God made Orunmila the custodian of all things in the world. It will be recalled that at the beginning of time, Orunmila was the only divinity who spied on God at creation. When God caught him spying, he quickly closed his eyes with his fingers like the other divinities were told to do. God however, told him to open his eyes and there-upon proclaimed Orunmila as his witness at creation. That was how he earned the sobriquet of (Eleri ipin in Yoruba or Ose N'Osanobua ya M'Ona in Bini). God told him that after knowing the secret of creation, he was from then on endowed with the authority to repair any creature that

Orunmila then sang in praise of the Almighty God in the following poem:

Oluwa Oniugbogbo ure, omure jimi;
Oyeku ba'turukpon,
Olomo Omu jimi
Oyeku ba turukpon,
Oloye, Oma Oye jimi
Oyeku ba turukpon
Oluwa Omu Ala jimi
Oyeku ba turukpon
Alaje Omu Aje jimi
Oyeku ba turukpon,
Onigbogbo Ure Omu re jimi.
Oyeku ba Turukpon.

OYEKU-LE-TURUKPON - When this odu comes out at divination and it forbodes danger (Ayewo in Yoruba or Ebe in Bini), it means a strong Awo is about to die. If he can be identified through further probing, he should be advised to make sacrifice quickly to the divinity of the Ground with a goat, an egg and 2 snails. It means that the elders of the night are plotting to kill a benevolent Awo. As soon as it appears at divination, you snap the thumb and the third finger — (Aghi suakpa fua) to ward off danger.

HOW OYEKU-LE-TURUKPON CAME TO THE WORLD:

At the divination he made before leaving heaven, he was told to make sacrifice to the ground with a goat, an egg and 2 snails to avoid premature death through the hands of stronger Awos on earth. He made the sacrifice. He turned out to be a very proficient Ifa Priest on earth. His success however soon earned him the envy and enmity of the more elderly Awos who began to plot for his demise.

When his guardian angel refused to surrender him for destruction, the enemies turned on his children. At that stage his guardian angel appeared to him in a dream and advised him to feast the elderly Awos (his enemies) with a goat after offering it as sacrifice to the Ground. He made a sumptuous feast. After the eating and drinking, the head of the Awos moved that they should all pray for him to survive the evil machinations of his enemies and ended up with a curse that anyone who dared to plan evil against him after the feast, should pay the prize with his own life. They advised him to continue to use his Ifa practice for the benefit of mankind. His main art of benevolence was to release the children of other people tied up by the elders of the night for elimination. He continued to do just that, and he also continued to have problems.

Meanwhile, he consulted Ifa who advised him to offer a he-goat to Esu. After eating his he-goat, Esu created confusion among his enemies, and they began to accuse one another in open confession. That was how the open confession by witches began. After the spate of confessions, his problems abated and he lived in peace and tranquility ever after.

HOW HE SOLVED THE PROBLEM OF WITCH-CRAFT:

When this Odu appears during an Ifa initiation ceremony at Ugbodu, the person should be warned that the elders of the night are going to be after him throughout his life. To be able to ride out the storm, he should immediately make a special sacrifice (Ono-Ifa in Yoruba or Ode-Iha in Bini) by digging the floor of his sitting room or bedroom and slaughtering a goat inside the hole with the appropriate leaves. The head of the goat together with an egg and 2 snails should be buried inside the hole.

That was the sacrifice which an Ifa Priest called OGBOMU GBOMU JA IJAJA-GBOMU advised Oyeku-le-Eturukpon to make when the elders of the night were after him. Thereafter, 2 birds or owls, which used to cry on the roof of his house every night stopped coming. One of the birds died and the other one flew away never to return. He was the Odu who scattered the cult of witch-craft when they plotted to destroy goodness and salvation in the world.

When this Odu appears at Ugbodu, the person will be told that owls or other mysterious birds used to cry near his compound in the night. He should make sacrifice with the head of a goat, an egg and 2 snails in the manner described above to solve the problem. If the person does not have a house of his own, he should fill a Box or a bucket with mud and bury inside it, the head of the goat, the egg and 2 snails and keep it safely in his room until it can be dug into the ground of his own house. If this special preparation is not made at Ugbodu, the person will surely die a premature death.

If the Odu appears at ordinary divination, the person should be advised to serve the Ground with an egg and 2 snails and to get an Ifa Priest to prepare the appropriate leaves to wash his head on a water-drain (Agba jomi in Yoruba or Uroramen in Bini).

HE MADE DIVINATION FOR CHILD-BIRTH:

There lived an over-aged spinster called Omojuola (Omosefe in Bini) who was barren.

Once upon a time, she travelled to the land of the muslims (Ilu Imole). She was herself a witch-doctor. When she got to the place, they told her that she was invited to the town because they were told at divination that she was the only one capable of helping them to restore peace and prosperity to the town. On the other hand, she replied that she agreed to come to the town because it was revealed to her that that was the only place she would live in, to have a child.

True to prediction, her arrival in the town marked the beginning of the return of peace and prosperity to the town of (Ilu-Imole). Soon afterwards, she missed her period and did not know that she was pregnant until three months later later when her breasts began to bulge. She had been cohabiting with a visiting Ifa Priest called Oyeku-Ba-turukpon. She had been to the Priest to make divination for her and Oyeku-ba-turukpon replied her initially with the following incantation after they fell in love with each other:

Mo de ile ki nki yin,
Mo ba yin ni 'le.
Mo bere ona titi.
Mi kori ona.
Esu Odara ni ofi
Ile re han mi
Alawo ni - fa gi re.

Meaning:
I came home to greet you, and
I met you at home.
I asked for the direction to your house
I could not locate it,
It was the good Esu who showed me your place,
Ifa became good to the awo.

She was advised to make sacrifice with 2 rabbits, 2 bags and 50k. The Priest told her that she would give birth to a child who should be named (IFAJIRE in Yoruba or IHASOGHOGHO in Bini). He also advised her to prepare a drum for the incoming child. She later gave birth to a male child who became a musician and she went to thank Ifa with the following song:

Ifa she mi loore - o
Oyeku-le-Eturukpon
Eni Tawo kekere - o
Oyeku-ba-Eturukpon
Ifa fi - re L'oni - o
Oyeku le eturukpon
Ifa she mi loore - o
Oyeku-le-eturukpon.

The son grew up to become a musician through which he enriched the parents.

At Ugbodu, the person will be told that he will initially have problems in having children. He should offer a black goat to Ifa, a black he-goat to Esu and a Pigeon to his head and he will start having children.

On the other hand, as soon as it appears at Ugbodu, the person will be told, that there is a pregnant woman around him whose pregnancy has not yet developed. For the pregnancy to develop, a drum should be prepared for the incoming child because he is going to be a musician.

At ordinary divination, the person should be told to serve Esu with a he-goat because he is an ingrate. He will be ungrateful to any Awo that helps him.

HOW OYEKU-BA-TURUKPON BECAME PROSPEROUS:

Although, he was a very proficient Ifa Priest, nonetheless, he just managed to make ends meet. One morning, he sounded Ifa and he was told that on account of the inability of the elders of the night to kill him or any of his children, they had tied up his fortune. He was told to make sacrifice with a duck to Ifa and that he should not eat any other part of the meat except the gizzard. He was also to offer a live rabbit and a melon (Elegede in Yoruba and Eyen in Bini) to the elders of the night. He made the sacrifice to Ifa, but searched in vain for a melon and a live rabbit. When he asked Ifa what to do, he was told to use a chicken to promise to give a he-goat to Esu, if he could help him to procure a rabbit and a melon. He gave the chicken to Esu.

Thereafter, he went to the bush one morning to fetch leaves for his work. In the forest, he came across a melon fruit and he took it. Soon afterwards, he came across a wounded rabbit and caught it. He subsequently came across two men who, unknown to him, were messengers from heaven. When they saw the rabbit and the melon in his hand, they begged him to surrender them. He refused on the ground that he came to the forest in search of a live rabbit and a melon for a special sacrifice in order to become prosperous. The two men besought him to name the price for the two materials because, they too were sent from heaven in search for the same materials.

Back in heaven, the daughter of ORISA-NLA was having a difficult labour and at divination, he was told that the elders of the night had held up the delivery unless sacrifice was made with a live Rabbit and a melon. Anxious to eat the he-goat promised by Oyeku-Ba-Turukpon on earth, Esu had ordered all the rabbits and melons of heaven to bury themselves beneath the earth. The followers of Orisa-Nla had combed the markets and forests of heaven in vain in search of the two materials and that is why they were sent to the earth where through telescopic telepathy they met Oyeku-Ba-Turukpon in the forest.

As he was about to name a price for the two materials, he was instantly possessed by Esu who influenced him to name the following as his price: 100 men, 100 women, 100 cows, 100 goats, 100 pieces of clothes, 100 bags of beads, and 100 bags of money.

Since the heavenly messengers did not have those things on them, they told him to give them the two materials and that before getting home, the price he named would be positioned in his house. He gave them the rabbit and the melon on trust and turned back to return home.

Instantly, the two messengers were back in heaven and the sacrifice was made and the daughter of Orisa-Nla made a safe delivery.

When the messengers narrated the price they promised to pay for the two materials, Orisa-nla ordered the price of the materials to appear in the home of Oyeku-Baturukpon on earth immediately.

The appearance of the materials in his house coincided with the time he got home which immediately translated him to prosperity. He immediately gave two he-goats to Esu instead of the single one he promised. He also made a big feast for the people of the town where he sang the song earlier sung by Omojuola.

    Ifa she mi loore - o
    Oyekun le-'turukpn
    Eni Tawo kekere - o
    Oyeku Ba-turukpon
    Ifa fi 're l'oni - o
    'Oyeku le 'turukpon
    Ifa she Mo'ere - o
    Oyeku le Eturukpon.

OYEKU-BA-TURUKPON
HE MADE DIVINATION FOR OLOFIN

    Gbo gbo re, gbo gbo re,
    Ifa ni yio bami she
    Adifa fun Olofin
    Omu koro mefa lowo she ni Odun.
    Ebo niki Agbekele Ifa.

That was the Awo who made divination for Olofin when six divine festivals fell due for him to celebrate simultaneously. He was required to perform at each of the six cults at the same time. When his Chiefs asked him how he was going to cope, he replied that Orunmila would help him to cope with the situation. He was told to make sacrifice to obtain the support of Orunmila. Thereafter, he performed the ceremonies without any hitch.

At divination, the person should be told to serve Orunmila in order to be able to cope with the six problems he has in hand.

HE MADE DIVINATION FOR IFASHEMOYIN

    Muso muso ni shuwaju ijo
    Gbeje gbeje ni gbehin ayo
    Adifa fun Ifashemoyin,
    Ti abi l'ode, to tun toni ode.
    Ofun le oko ni ode,
    Ebo lo ma ru.

Meaning: When entering a dance, the dancer,
    Brings his hands forward in anticipation.
    After dancing successfully, the dancer,

Brings his hands down as a mark,
Of achievement before sitting down.

These were the Awos who made divination for Ifashemoyin before she settled down to live in the town of Ode. Although her parents did not hail from the land of Ode, she was born, was raised, lived, and happily married there. That was because she had made sacrifice in order to live and prosper in the land of Ode.

At divination, the person should be told that he is not a native of the town where he or she lives. The person should however, make sacrifice because, his prosperity lies in the town.

THE POEM FOR PROSPERITY:

Oju shemi kimi wi
Adifa fun moburin burin,
 Moye ikin mi wo,
Omo kekere Awo nifi okpon ide di ifa.
Aha ha hi ri hi ri
Oshi shi shiri shiri,
Adifa fun Orunmila,
 O'nfa ologbe - ure le rele
Akokpore lowo ati aye ero,
Ebo ki asin tun bo ifa,
Ifa mowa lowore
Okpe maje kimi juya.

Meaning: I had an inclination,
 To go for divination,
 I later felt like sounding,
 The ikin tied to my waist, and;
 Using it to make divination.
 I later met a young Ifa priest,
 Who used brass tray for divination.
 Full of youthful exuberance and fervour
 I finally asked him for divination.
 Before going to befriend prosperity, and
 cajole him to the homes of my practising Ifa
  Priest.
 The sacrifice is done by serving,
 Orunmila and telling him,
  Okpe, I am in your hands,
 For deliverance and salvation,
 Do not allow me to suffer.

That was how Orunmila gave his followers the indication that any Ifa Priest who follows his ways of kindness and purity, will be aptly compensated by him. An Ifa priest who hides behind Orunmila, to extort money from suffering humanity, can never become prosperous. On the other hand, an Ifa priest who follows the path of Orunmila by making modest demands, and even spending his own money to fund the sacrifices required to be made by destitute clients, will be compensated ten-fold. Orunmila will gradually drag prosperity to his home.

When this Odu appears at divination for a young man who is anxious to know what profession he is destined to follow, he should be told to learn the art and practice of Ifism. He should be told categorically that he is an Ifa Priest and that he will only prosper through the honest and dedicated followership of Orunmila.

HE MADE DIVINATION TO WARD-OFF DEATH.

Olu ga, nga,
Ode ka ka taa,
Adafa fun oyeku tori iku.
Ebo akii sa ati kara hun igbin
Iku, jekimi jo hanre,
Oyeku ba 'turukpon,
Iku je 'njo hanre
Oyeku ba 'turukpon.

These were the two awos who made divination for Oyeku when death was hovering over him. He was told to make sacrifice with rags, which he was to wear on his body. At the same time, he was to sew up snails' shells round his body, and that when death came for him, he should seek his permission to dance for him before killing him.

When death eventually came, Oyeku asked for and obtained permission to dance for his entertainment. He wore the rags and snails' shells and began to dance to the accompaniment of clapping hands, while he sang:-

Uku jenjo hunre
Oyeku ba 'turukpon.
Refrain.

When death saw him dancing, he burst into laughter and left him alone to continue to live on earth.

If this Odu comes out as Ayewo, that is, if it forbodes danger at divination, he should be told that death is on his trail, and that if he becomes ill, he will die unless he makes sacrifice with a sheep, snails and rags.

He will make a similar garment in rags and snails' shells and dance in it with members of his house-hold clapping and singing from the Ifa shrine up to Esu shrine, where, the garment will be removed. If the divination however foretells or foresees no danger (Ure), the person should nonetheless make sacrifice with he-goat to Esu.

Chapter 15
OYEKU - OSE
OYEKU - KPA - EKU - OSE

```
  I    II
  II   II
  I    II
  II   II
```

It was this Odu that revealed the strength of the divinity of Fear, who is reputed to be the most dreaded divinity created by God. Although, he has no shrine or followership, he is nonetheless dreaded by all other divine, mortal and other animate creatures of God. It is the divinity of Fear that prepares the minds of other creatures of God before any other divinity strikes. Any one who feels threatened by any unwanted incident such as failure, death, sickness, imprisonment, the unknown judgement etc. becomes the victim of the divinity of Fear before the event or non-event, which makes Fear the most powerful force created by God. The strength of Fear is aptly demonstrated by the following revelation made by Oyeku-Ose

HOW ORUNMILA MARRIED IRE THE DAUGHTER OF GOD.

Ire or the good tidings created by God was the only daughter in the divine household of God, but no divinity knew what to do with her. It was Esu who revealed to the divinities the purpose for which she or the fair sex was created; that is, for the purpose of procreation. God did not reveal it to the divinities. That is what biblical mythology refers to as the temptation of man. The first book on Ifism revealed how Esu inserted the genitals between the legs of human beings. It will be recalled that even the divinities were created with the same physical features with which man was later endowed.

As soon as the divinities knew the sensual and conjugal significance of Ire, they began to troop to God for her hand in marriage. At that time, the earth had been created and the wickedness of the people of the world was already being reported in heaven. God responded by telling the divinities that any of them who could deliver the heads of 200 wicked human beings or followers of evil, from the earth would be given Ire for marriage. Death and Ogun, the only two divinities capable of killing human beings frontally, boasted that the contest was between the two of them. They promised to deliver the skulls of 200 evil doers within three days. Orunmila who neither had the inclination nor the physical ability to kill, however, decided to ask his Ifa whether he could contest for the hand of Ira. He was advised to offer a he-goat to Esu and to serve Fear with 201 snails. He did as he was told. Ifa also advised him to leave very early the next morning after the sacrifice, and hide at the boundary of heaven and earth.

Meanwhile, Death left for earth in the company of his wife (ARUN) or Sickness, to fetch 200 human heads. At the same time Ogun also left for the earth. Death took his wife along in the hope of making a quick job of accomplishing his task because, he can only strike at one person at a time with his club. On the other hand, his wife, Sickness is capable of crippling and killing many persons at the same time. On his part, Ogun is capable of multiple killings simultaneously.

After eating his he-goat, Esu went to the divinity of Fear and told him to work in favour of Orunmila for the snails offered to him. The divinity of Fear sowed up the shells of the 201 snails which Orunmila gave him on a fork-stick and took position at the boundary between heaven and earth.

Meanwhile, Ogun and Death had left for earth to fetch their victims which they lost no time in procuring. Before then, no one knew the Modus Operandi of the divinity of Fear nor how to anticipate its manifestation. As soon as Fear knew that Death and Ogun were approaching the boundary of heaven and earth, he took the fork-stick containing the 201 snails' shells and began to sing the following song:

Bi maruku mabaja,
Iworiwo ji, Iworiwo ji wowo
Bi marogun ma gbe de,
Iworiwo ji, Iworiwo ji wowo
Bi mori arun mabaja
Iworiwo ji, Iworiwo ji wowo.

With that war song, Fear was boasting with brazen bravado that whenever he came across Death, Ogun, and Sickness, he would fight them to finish. Orunmila who had meanwhile, taken position at Erebus, the dark zone between heaven and earth through which everyone passes on their way to Hades, over-heard the strange song of the unknown combatant without knowing who he was.

As Ogun, Death and Sickness approached the boundary of heaven and earth, they heard the strange war cry and they began to wonder who it was that was threatening them with such ferocity and impunity. Ogun, who was in front, pondered that any force who dared to boast to tie him up in chains, was surely capable of disgracing him. He immediately dropped his luggage of 200 human skulls and raced back in fright towards the earth. Death and his wife reacted in like manner after hearing the boastful song.

Back in his hide-out, Orunmila was approached by Esu who told him to collect the luggages dropped by Ogun and Death and make with them straight to the palace of God. To this day, none of them saw the face of the divinity of Fear, although, Orunmila was satisfied that his sacrifice did minifest. When Orunmila got to the palace of God, he reported that he decided to come with twice as many human skulls as He demanded because of the special significance of the prospect of marrying Ire, the daughter of God. God immediately betrothed Ire to Orunmila. It was not until the following day that Ogun came back with his own 200 skulls, but God told him hat Orunmila had already beaten him to it. The next day, Death reported with his own load of human skulls and he got the same reply. That was how Orunmila procured the support of the faceless divinity of Fear to win the contest with Death and Ogun for the hands of Ire the daughter of God.

It is important to note that Orunmila has since adopted the war song chanted by Fear on that day when he is trying to scare off a ferocious enemy.

When this Odu appears at Ugbodu, the person will be told that he is proposing to marry a wife and that he has two rivals stronger than himself to contend with. He should therefore serve Ifa with 16 snails and sew up the shells of the snails to a fork-stick and hit the ground with it from the Ifa shrine to the shrine of Esu, singing the above mentioned song. If he does the sacrifice, he will win the hands of the Lady. On the other hand, if it comes out at divination, the person will be told that he is about to embark on a difficult mission capable of ending his life. He should serve; Esu with a he-goat, and serve Ifa with 16 snails, if he is to survive the mission.

HE ALSO MADE DIVINATION FOR THE OAK TREE:

Egungun okeere,
Odun wiwo bi aba de idi re
Sisun ni Isun ni,
Odifa fun Egungun Ono Oja.
The oak tree is beautiful,
When viewed from the distance,
But big as one gets near to it.

That was the name of the Ifa priest who made divination for the Oak-tree on the road to the market when he was lamenting that he had no followership. The Oak tree was advised to make sacrifice with a hen, snails, pigeon and calico cloth. He made the sacrifice. Meanwhile, the sun was shining intensely when people were returning from the market. They began to take rest and shelter under the Oak tree. In that way, he began to receive many visitors.

When this Odu comes out at divination, the person should be told that he has no followership. He should make a similar sacrifice and his tide would turn for the better.

HE ALSO MADE DIVINATION FOR ORISA-NLA OSHERE-IGBO

One of Orisa-Nla's children was very troublesome. He went for divination and was told to wash the head of that son on the road to the market in order to do well in life. He did the sacrifice and the son began to progress in life.

At divination, the person should be told that he has one son who is giving him a lot of anxiety. He should give a piece of white cloth to one divinity he has in his house or family. He should also look for an Ifa Priest to prepare leaves to wash the head of the son either on Esu shrine or on the way to the market.

HE ALSO MADE DIVINATION FOR THE BROWN RAT (EKU-OLOSE or EKU-OMO IN YORUBA OR EKUOMO IN BINI):

Omo lakoko gun mori ga ade
Odifa fun Eku Olose tabi eku emo
Ni jo to'nfi omi oju shubere
Omo tuurutu.

The rat was anxious to have children and went for divination. He was told to make

sacrifice and he did and began to have children. Thereafter, he began to rejoice with the following song:
> Eku Loshe Are mo te
> Te te - o, Aremo - which is its cry to this day after having children.

OYEKU-OSE LEAVES FOR EARTH:

Before leaving heaven, he went for divination and his own Odu appeared. He was told to make sacrifice with a he-goat to Esu in order to avoid coming in contact with, or marrying a woman stronger than himself on earth. He did not bother to do the sacrifice. He then left for earth. While on earth, he took to Ifa art and practice. One day, he travelled to the town of Ilode for Ifa practice. He was otherwise a very proficient Ifa priest. He received many clients at Ilode and he succeeded in solving all their probems. Two days before he returned home, he met a young lady who came to him to find out what to do in order to have the right husband. It was the news of his success in helping others to solve their problems, that induced the lady to come to him. Unknown to him, the girl was the daughter of Olokun who came to the market from heaven.

At divination, he told her to serve Esu with a he-goat. The Odu which came out for the girl was his own Ifa — that is, Oyeku-Ose. The Ifa also indirectly reminded him of the sacrifice to Esu which he failed to make before leaving heaven, but he ignored it.

On her part, the girl promised to make the sacrifice on the next market day. As evening was already approaching, the woman appealed to him to give her a place in his lodging to spend the night. He agreed to accommodate her for the night. The lady asked him where she was to meet him for the sacrifice on the next market day. He had meanwhile, after divination, told the girl that she would only prosper in life if she married a practicing Ifa priest. She returned home the next morning after giving her the description of his house at Oke-Mesi in Ife.

The following day, he returned home with all the gifts and remunerations he received at Ilu-Ode. Four days later, the woman followed his description and came to his house at Oke-Mesi. After performing the sacrifice for her she professed love to him and he agreed to marry her. The woman began immediately to live with him in his house without bothering to find out where she came from. However, he soon discovered that she neither knew how to cook nor how to take care of the house because she was used to having those chores performed for her by the domestic servants in her parent's house. He soon became dis-illusioned and did not know what to do with her. She also proved to be totally insubordinate when she discovered that she could not subdue the husband.

One night, his guardian angel appeared to him and sang the following song to him:-
> Ka ibi emi maa gbe yi ri
> Amebo Olokun yei yei
> Ekpe - o ariro.

That was how his guardian angel came to reveal to him that he was toying with the daughter of Olokun.

The following morning, Esu visited him under the guise of an Ifa Priest to make divination for him. Esu reminded him of the he-goat he had been told ever so often to give to Esu. The visitor insisted that he must perform the sacrifice immediately. He produced a he-goat and the Ifa Priest used the blood and the head of the he-goat to wash his head on the shrine of Esu. After performing the sacrifice, the Ifa Priest went away with the he-goat. That was how the tradition began in which a person who uses a he-goat to wash his head on the shrine of Esu is not allowed to eat out of its meat because, the Ifa Priest who peroframed the sacrifice traditionally goes home with the he-goat, just as Esu went away with Oyeku's-Ose's he-goat.

After eating his he-goat, Esu went back to heaven to persuade the other divinities to admonish Olokun for allowing the daughter to perform so reprehensibly in the home of Orunmila on earth. Olokun apologised to them and promised to send a message to his daughter to refrain from misbehaving to Orunmila. All the divinities agreed to intercede in favour of Orunmila because of the salvation he was offering to the children of the world.

Olokun subsequently invited his daughter back to heaven and kept her in solitary confinement for seven-days for her misbehaviour not only to her husband, but also for escaping from his palace in heaven to marry on earth without his blessing. After serving the seven day imprisonment, she apologised to her father and begged to be allowed to rejoin her husband because, she had deeply fallen in love with him. Thereafter, the father prepared her fully for proper settlement in her husband's home and sent her back with servants and maids together with all items of prosperity required for living a prosperous life on earth. By the time she got back to her husband, she had changed tremendously for the better, and the instruments of treasure she returned with, made the couple exceedingly wealthy ever after. She subsequently had seven children for her husband all of who turned out to be responsible men and women.

When this Odu appears at Ugbodu or divination, the man will be told that he owes a debt of sacrifice respectively to Esu and Olokun. He will be told that his wife is from the palace of Olokun. If he does not give a he-goat to Esu and make sacrifice to Olokun, the wife will die. But if he makes these sacrifices, she will make him prosper.

HE MADE DIVINATION FOR A BARREN WOMAN:

One day, after Oyeku-Ose started having children, a barren woman visited him for divination. The woman was otherwise very wealthy. At divination Oyeku-Ose sang the following poem before speaking to the woman:-

    Ifa Oyeku Ose,
    Ise ni la nse,
    Ki a to le ko Ifa.
    Iya ni la nje
    Ki a to

    le mo ibogbi-gba
    Ti a ba se ise tan

Ti a ba fi ko Ifa
A - o - wa di eni nla
Ti a ba mo Ibo - gbi gba tan
Won a wa ki eni ni kpele omo Awo.

Meaning: Thanks to Ifa Oyeku-Ose
We have to put in more effort at work
To enable us study Ifa art.
We encountered some difficulties,
Before understanding the art of making
sacrifice.
After the days work, and having utilized it,
for the study of Ifa art,
Then shall we become great and prosperous.
At the end of having understood the art of
making sacrifice.
There will be praises and calling of names
as Omo-Awo.

Orunmila disclosed to the woman that she was anxious to have a child and assured her that she would have a child if she could promise appropriate compensation to Orunmila. The woman in reply said that she was so rich that she had everything that money could buy, except a child. She then promised that If Orunmila succeeded in helping her to have a child, she would share all her belongings into two and surrender one part to him. Orunmila told her to produce a pregnant sheep (Ewe) for sacrifice. The sacrifice was made and the following month, the woman became pregnant. In the fullness of time, she gave birth to a male child. The woman subsequently had two other children in quick succession before getting to menopause.

If this Odu appears at divination for a woman, she will be told that she is itching to have a child. If it comes out for a man, he should be told that he has an insubordinate wife who is anxious to have a child. In either case, the person should be advised to make sacrifice with a pregnant sheep and the woman will start having children.

HE MADE DIVINATION FOR THE FARMER: OYEKU-KPEKU OSE

There lived a farmer who held meetings with the elders of the night. He used to plant melon or Ogiri in his farm. When his melon were ripe for harvesting, a swarm of mice descended on the farm and began to eat up the crops. He immediately reported the incident to the elders of the night, who advised him to prepare a special pot with the leaves of the sand-paper plant (ewe - ukpin in yoruba and Ebe-ame-men in Bini). He was advised to put one cowry inside the pot and to position it in his farm. Unknown to them, the invading rats belonged to Orunmila. The next time the rats went to ravage the farm, they were ensnared to drink out of the water in the pot. As soon as they did so, they began to die. When Orunmila discovered that most of his rats were dead, he went to the farmer to ask him what he gave to his rats. The farmer explained that when he discovered that the rats were eating up his crops, he appealed to the elders of the night who helped him to prepare the pot which killed them. Orunmila became infuriated. The following night, he went outside his house and with his left knee on the ground, repeated the following incantation:-

 Ebubu Ewara
  Aboju boge
 Akpa maa nkpekun
  Otoro mo fi Iyo
  Oruko ton kpeye
 Oba lu-gbagba lo-otun
  Oba lu-gbagba lo-osi
  Koye ko kpeku
  Koye ko kpe eja
  Ire la ani koo ko.

At that point in time, the witches were already assembled for their nightly meeting. As soon as Orunmila finished repeating the incantation, there was pandemonium at the meeting of the witches, as they began to fight among themselves. Meanwhile, a male and female delegation of the witches raced to Orunmila's house to apologise to him and to beg for forgiveness. He agreed to forgive them but warned them never again to destroy anything belonging to him.

At Ugbodu, the person should be advised to offer a black hen and nine eggs as sacrifice to the night so that they might stop spoiling his belongings. He should ask his Oluwo to prepare night Ogun for his Ifa to ward off any danger from the night. At divination, the person should make quick sacrifice to the night so that the favour coming to him might not pass him by to someone else. He will be told that there are rats spoiling his things in his house. He should prepare sand-paper leaves (Ebamenmen) into a pot, adding the cowry and the divination powder (Iyerosun) of Oyeku-Ose, and therefore, And the rats will surely die. He can soak the meat of rat and fish with the water from the pot, before using them to bait the rats.

That is how this Odu earned his name of OYEKU-KPA-EKU-OSE.

OYEKU-KPA-KIN-OSE REVEALS HOW ORUNMILA GOT MARRIED TO THE WORLD:

 Oye lotun oye losi,
 Adafa fun Orunmila
 Ni jo ti ofe gbe Aiye shaya
 Ni ibere igba.

This Odu reveals how Orunmila succeeded in marrying the world, (Aiye) the only daughter of God at the beginning of time. When God created the divinities, he did not disclose to them how to make use of their genitals. They did not therefore know the significance of the penis and the vulva. It was Esu who later revealed to the penis and the vulva the motive for which they were created by God, other than for respiratory purposes. As soon as the divinities knew the pleasures of the genitals, it was only then that they appreciated the conjugal significance of the differing features of Aiye, the only woman created by God. One after the other, beginning with Ogun - the divinities went to God to beseech Him for the hands of Aiye as a life partner. God told them one after the other to approach her and that if she consented, he would have no objection.

Whenever they approached Aiye however, she vowed that she would only marry the divinity who succeeded in knowing her secret or in seeing her genitals in the nude. That was an impossible task because, she neither bathed nor dressed in presence of any one.

After all the other divinities had tried and failed, they challenged Orunmila to make an effort which he was reluctant to do because, he did not imagine how he could succeed where others had failed. He however invited all the Awos to his left, and to his right, for divination.

After divination, he was told to make sacrifice which he was to carry by himself after midnight, to the river in the heart of the forest of heaven. The following day, he collected the materials for the sacrifice and it was prepared by all the Awos. As soon as he made sure that all living creatures had slept, that is, after midnight, he carried the sacrifice and left for the river in the middle of the forest in total darkness.

When he eventually got to the river, he knelt down by the bank and held the sacrifice on both hands and began to pray. He prayed that he had come to make the sacrifice in order to be able to see the genitals of Aiye, the daughter of God in the nude because, he wanted to marry her. Unknown to him however, that was the very point and time at which Aiye was having her nocturnal bath, although, he did not see her.

As he was praying, Aiye exclaimed:-
Orunmila, oti ri ihohò mi ni gbehin,
Iwo nikan lo ri idi Aiye,
Iwo nikan loma gbe Aiye shaya.
Meaning:
Orunmila, you have at last,
seen my genitals in the nude.
Thus, you are the only divinity,
That has known the secret of the world,
And therefore, the only one
Who can have her as a wife.

She embraced Orunmila and dressed up at once to go with him to the palace of God, where she proclaimed him as her eternal husband. That event explains the reason why Orunmila remains the only divinity that knows the secrets of the world.

At divination, the person should be told to have his own Ifa without any delay. If the divination is made in connection with a proposed marriage, the man should be told to have his own Ifa before approaching the woman, if he is to succeed in marrying her. If the man is already married however, he should nonetheless, be told to have his own Ifa because, the new marriage will transform him into fame and fortune. If it is a woman making the enquiry for marriage, she should be told that she is the wife of Orunmila and will only succeed in life if she marries a man having his own Ifa, unless she can persuade the suitor to have his own Ifa before marrying her.

Author's Special note
It is necessary to resolve the similarity between the fore-going passage on Aiye and the first passage of this Chapter on Ire. They are simply two different sides of the same coin, having been revealed by separate authorities on the subject.

MADE DIVINATION TO RESTORE THE CONFIDENCE OF OKE AFTER OTHER AWOS TOLD HIM HE WOULD NEVER PROSPER:

Igun ko gbo ohun orun. Awodi ko gban omi eja. The vulture failed to listen to the voice of heaven and Awodi tried to catch fish without bailing water.

These were the two diviners who made divination for Oke when he was advised to discard his Ifa because he was never going to prosper. He left their place in tears and cried his way home, until he met other Awos called: A bogunde, the Ifa priest from Egbaland; Asagede, the Ifa priest of Ijesha, Akpa Koko in Koko t'nko ogban ikin lowo da ni oju okpan, the Awo who made Ikin divination with thirty instead of sixteen seeds.

The three Awos asked him why he was crying and he explained that some diviners had advised him to throw away his Ifa (Ikin) because he was never going to prosper in life. Asked for the Odu that appeared for him during the divination, he replied that it was Oyeku-Kpeku-Ose.

They however re-assured him that he would prosper provided he was able to make sacrifice with a ram, eku-emo and the clothes he was wearing. He went to borrow money to make the sacrifice. Three months later, he became so prosperous that he married two wives at same time, began to have children and repaid the loan, built his own house and bought a horse for his trading business. Three years after the sacrifice he was given a chieftaincy title. He made a feast to which he invited the two sets of Awos who made contradictory divinations for him. He sang in praise of his Ifa and the last three Awos who made the sacrifice that brought him eternal prosperity.

When this Ifa appears at Ugbodu, the person will be forewarned that he is likely to meet some seers, most probably, Christian visionaries, who will advise him to discard his Ifa. He should seek a second opinion before abiding by their advice. If it appears at divination, the person will be told that he should arrange to have his own Ifa if he is to prosper. He should not listen to any doom and gloom diviners, visionaries or seers.

Chapter 16
OYEKU - OFUN
OYEKU - WO - LE - OFUN
OYEKU - YA - FUN - OKU,

Not much is known about the heavenly works of Oyeku-Ofun. Orunmila however, promised to make subsequent revelations which would later appear in the revised edition of this book if the writer lives long enough to do so.

Before leaving heaven however, Oyeku-Ofun went to two Awos for divination of what to do for a successful sojourn on earth. The names of the Ifa Priests were:- Ojo ungbo ti oro; and Ojo ungbo ti Oro. He was advised to make sacrifice because everybody he came across was going to cheat him on earth. He was told to make sacrifice with a tortoise, but refused to do it. He subsequently came to the world where he took to farming with the name of Ero. He mainly planted yams in his farm which yielded prolific harvests. The good harvest from his farm coincided with generally bad harvests for other farmers in that particular year. He was the only one who had yams available for sale in his arm.

Meanwhile, a man called IJAPA hatched a plan for stealing yams from his farm. He prepared a rectangular basket with a wooden base (akpere in Yoruba and agban in Bini) with which Ijapa used to steal yams from Ero's farm. after loading the container with yams, he would cover it with a white cloth to make it look like a coffin and would start singing: Joungbo ti oro, Joungbo ti oro. Eniyan mefa, Loun ku loko Ero. Oun logbe lo ori eyi Ko ya fun Oku. Meaning: Six persons have died today in Ero's farm. Those who forbid to see corps, should hide their faces away. Meanwhile, the people farming for Ero began to wonder who was stealing yams from their farm. They appealed to Ogun and Orunmila who refused to go because, they forbid to see human corpse. Ero then went to Orunmila for divination on what to do apprehend the thief. He was advised to serve Esu with he-goat and to make sacrifice with a tortoise. The tortoise was used to serve Osanyin or Osun-nake. He made the sacrifices.

After eating his tortoise, Osanyin parceled himself with leaves and concealed himself behind the farm barn of Ero's farm. The next day, Ijapa again came to the farm, loaded his container with yams and once more, covered it with white cloth.

As he turned to return home, he saw a small parcel behind the barn and picked it up. As he opened it, he found a small image of Osanyin or sigidi inside the parcel.

Osanyin instantly accused him of stealing and pierced his magic wand (Uranke) into the anus of Ijapa. That wand is the tail at the anus of the tortoise to this day. On getting home, under Osanyin's escort, he was tried before court of elders, found guilty of robbery and executed.

When this Odu comes out at divination, if the person does not already have children, he should be told to make sacrifice to avoid problems in having children. If he already has children, he should also make sacrifice to avoid losing them one after the other.

HE MADE DIVINATION FOR EWE-EBIBA or (EBIEBA IN BINI)

Before leaving heaven, Ewe-Ebiba was advised to make sacrifice, and to refrain from making friends on earth, in order to obviate the risk of being used and later discarded by ingrates. She did not make the sacrifice.

On getting to the world, she was befriending all kinds of women especially fair complexioned ones.

They however began to use her for wrapping Eko (Akasan), Ekuru (Emieki) and moyin-moyin (Emieki-ere). After using her for their trading purposes, she was often discarded and cast away. That is the fate of Ewe-Ebiba to this day, on account of the sacrifice she failed to make in heaven.

When she is being used to wrap any pudding, and being unfolded before being discarded, she sings in remembrance of the Awos who made divination for her in heaven who were as follows:-

Agbon Omi ni jujo Ori igi,
Ade biiti ni jujo Eba Ona,
Won difa fun gbongbon gi Iya,
To 'ko ori igi si ile, To lob eko ati ekuru sho 're.

When it comes out at divination for a woman, she should be advised not to leave her husband to avoid becoming useless like the Ewe-Ebiba used for wrapping Eko and Ekuru.

HE MADE DIVINATION FOR A YOUNG HORSE RIDER:

A young man who was still learning how to ride on a horse soon began to boast that he was capable of defeating the popular Jockey in the town. When the Jockey was told about the challenge from the young man, he sent words to him to learn more horse riding before challenging him to a contest, because, a toddler cannot win a race with an adult. The young man went for divination to:

Yaa a fun Oku, Yaa fun Eniyan, Gbirigidi lu koto.

He was told not to risk the contest, but that if he was determined to go ahead, he should offer a he-goat to Esu to avoid sudden death in the process. Since he had no laurels to win from the race, even if he won it, he saw no justifiable reason for having to go into the heavy expense of buying a he-goat for sacrifice. Without heeding the advice of the Awos, he went ahead to formally challenge the Jockey to a race. When the contest began, Esu to whom he refused to make any sacrifice, quickly went to his trail, pushed him and he fell down, dead.

When it comes out at divination for a man, he should be warned not to embark on a venture he is determined to risk, especially if it resolves into a boastful challenge of a more elderly person. He will not win the contest, but if he must go through with it, he must offer a he-goat to Esu before doing so in order to avoid the risk of sudden death.

OYEKU-YA-FUN-OKU:

Oyeku and Ofun were close friends:
Ifa Oyeku wo ile ofun,
Igba nala ni,
O nlu kiji ka inu oko.

Oyeku was told to make sacrifice with a big he-goat to be buried on the ground to avoid death to a close friend. He did not do the sacrifice. Meanwhile, Oyeku went on a visit to Ofun's house. As he sat down in the house, he saw people carrying the corpse of Ofun into the house having died in the farm. Oyeku quickly turned his face to another direction having been warned never to see a human corpse. That was how this Odu got the sobriquet of

OYEKU-YA-FUN-OKU.

If it comes out at divination or at Ugbodu, the person will be told that someone close to him will die suddenly but that he should endeavor to avoid seeing the corpse. He should make sacrifice so that the dead of a close relation is not brought to his house.

HE MADE DIVINATION FOR A TRADER:

A cloth trader went to Orunmila to find out what to do to flourish in his business. He was advised to offer he-goat to Esu. He was also told to make a small drum with the skin of the he-goat and to always put the drum within his cloth-wares when going to the market. He made the sacrifice.

As soon as the skin of the he-goat dried up, he used it to prepare a small drum which he kept within the load of clothes he was going to sell in the market. The following day, as he was going to the market, he was accosted by three armed bandits. Asked where he was going, he replied that he was on his way to the market to sell his merchandise of cloths. They requested him to give them one piece of cloth each but he refused. They retorted by seizing the entire merchandise from him and left for the ware-house where they kept the loot of their robberies in the heart of the forest. When they got to the ware-house, they put down the parcel of cloths but to their amazement, something began to sing the following song from within the luggage:-

asho tiege tiege tori boo
asho tiege tiege tori boo
Osho geregere tori boo.

Which happened to be the names of the three bandits. Out of fright and curiosity, they opened the parcel of cloth and found the talking drum that had been singing with their names. As soon as they saw the drum, a boa (Oka or Arumwoto) came out of the drum and bit each of them. As they pursued the boa to kill it, each of them dropped dead.

Meanwhile, the trader went to Orunmila to find out what to do about the three bandits who had robbed him. In fact, he accused Orunmila of cheating him by advising him to make a sacrifice which only manifested in mis-adventure. Orunmila kept his cool and after divination, advised him to return home at once because he would soon recover his stolen wares at a premium. He never knew what Orunmila meant.

The trader returned home with mixed feelings. Not long afterwards, he heard a voice calling on his name at the back of his house. When he went out to verify who was hailing on his name, he found the small drum which he kept within his merchandise, dancing in circles and commanding him to follow him back into the forest. He accordingly followed the direction of the drum which led him first to the corpses of the three dead bandits and later to their forest ware-house.

Not only did he retrieve his cloths, he also inherited the entire loots of the robbers in the ware-house. He packed everything to his house which consisted of all imaginable goods of value and money. The unexpected find made him so rich that he was later given a high chieftaincy title in the town.

When this Odu comes out at Ugbodu, the person should be told to give a big he-goat to Esu, and to use the skin to prepare a drum which he will put on the shrine of his Ifa if he has one. If he does not already have Ifa, he should arrange to be initiated into Ifism because, Orunmila would bring prosperity to him. At ordinary divination, the person should be told to make the same sacrifice and warned that he would become the victim of an imminent robbery. If he makes the sacrifice, the robbery will surely become a blessing in disguise.

www.ingramcontent.com/pod-product-compliance
Lightning Source LLC
Chambersburg PA
CBHW022108160426
43198CB00008B/399